BRIDGE TIPS

FROM THE

MASTERS

BRIDGE TIPS

FROM THE

MASTERS

EDITED BY TERENCE REESE

Introduction by RICHARD L. FREY, Editor Emeritus
of the American Contract Bridge League Bulletin

A HERBERT MICHELMAN BOOK
CROWN PUBLISHERS, INC.
NEW YORK

INQUIRIES SHOULD BE ADDRESSED TO CROWN PUBLISHERS, INC.,
ONE PARK AVENUE, NEW YORK, NEW YORK 10016

PRINTED IN THE UNITED STATES OF AMERICA

PUBLISHED SIMULTANEOUSLY IN CANADA BY
GENERAL PUBLISHING COMPANY LIMITED

LIBRARY OF CONGRESS CATALOGING IN PUBLICATION DATA
MAIN ENTRY UNDER TITLE:

BRIDGE TIPS FROM THE MASTERS.

"A HERBERT MICHELMAN BOOK."
INCLUDES INDEX.
1. CONTRACT BRIDGE—ADDRESSES, ESSAYS, LECTURES.
I. REESE, TERENCE.
GV1282.3.B744   1981   795.41'53   81-4497
                                      AACR2
ISBN: 0-517-544644

10 9 8 7 6 5 4 3 2 1

FIRST EDITION

CONTENTS

INTRODUCTION

I got my first "tip" on play in 1923, when I was eighteen. The game was auction. For more than a year I had been winning consistently and not insubstantially, so I considered myself pretty good. Then a young newcomer joined the game and quite early in our first partnership, he had occasion to scream, "Idiot! Haven't you ever heard of the 'Rule of Eleven'?" Well, perhaps he didn't actually scream, but the Rule of Eleven became firmly seared into my mind, along with the realization that there was much to learn before I could really consider myself a good player.

How I wish that this book, or even one remotely approaching it, had been available in the next seven years. But it would have been impossible to find such a book then because most of the tips you will get here were unknown and the rest were the jealously guarded secrets of the few experts of that day.

Why seven years? Because that was how long I toiled—happily and profitably, I admit, but toiling nevertheless—before I won my first major bridge championship, the Goldman Pairs, playing with the late Geoffrey Mott-Smith. He was still teaching me things when we nosed out the defending title-holders, Oswald Jacoby and George Reith.

In the interim, I had learned contract, joined Mott-Smith's Embassy Club, and begun to play the duplicate circle in clubs like the famous old Knickerbocker, where Sidney Lenz, Ely Culbertson, Howard Schenken, Jacoby and Reith, and a few other of the early greats had long been the big-time stars. Duplicate was, and still is, the best and cheapest way to play against better players, to observe what they do and why they do it.

You hear it said that there is little new in the play of the cards since Ely Culbertson's *Red Book*, Louis Watson's *Play of the Hand*, and, more recently, Charles Goren's *Play and Defense*, all excellent books from which to learn the fundamentals of skill. Compared to the revolutions in bidding, this is partly true. *Partly.*

But, to borrow from Shakespeare: "There are more things in heaven and earth, Horatio, than are dreamt of in your philosophy." A good cardplayer who learned in the late '20s and early '30s will still be a good player—until he is thrown into the arena with today's top stars. Then, if he has not kept up with the kind of "tips" to be found in this book, he will be eaten alive.

The first year, 1974, the IBPA chose the invitees and appointed to judge the entries a jury that eventually grew to thirty internationally famous experts.

The results were privately circulated to all members of the IBPA, and the resulting publicity—in nineteen languages!—as well as the caliber of the tips were so far beyond expectations that Bols renewed their sponsorship in each of the two succeeding years. (The Bols Company continues to sponsor different forms of competition under the aegis of the IBPA.)

Long before the competition had run its allotted three-year course, the IBPA began to receive a flood of requests that the tips be enlarged and developed, and published in book form. The choice of the authority to perform this task was not difficult. As a service to IBPA and to the world of bridge, Terence Reese, a former world champion and a brilliant theorist, regarded by many of his peers as the world's outstanding bridge writer, agreed to do the book. As you will see, he has done his customary masterful job of making even the most arcane tips clear and readily understandable to any student of the game.

The IBPA owes thanks to the many members who helped to make this book possible, to the contestants and to the judges, all of whom shared in its creation. It especially owes its gratitude to the Bols Company, to Herman Filarski, and to Albert Dormer, editor of the *IBPA Bulletin* and a leading member of the executive committee, who provided much help at every stage, but particularly in the tasks of producing this book and presenting it to the British publisher, Robert Hale.

When you have read these tips, I am sure you

will agree that they earn more than enough congratulations to go around to all who helped to make this unique volume possible, including the American producer, Harold H. Hart, long an avid and serious bridge player, who quickly recognized its value and who arranged to have it published simultaneously with its initial presentation at the World Bridge Olympiad in Valkenburg, Holland, in 1980.

Richard L. Frey

RICHARD L. FREY

*Dick Frey, one of the youngest of the early contract
bridge greats, has won virtually every major American
national tournament title, some of them more than once.
He was eighth in the first group to be created a Life
Master of the American Contract Bridge League, and an
original member of The Four Aces, the team that swept
the American team championships in 1933 and 1934, the
year when he had the best tournament record of all
American players and coauthored* The Four Aces System
of Contract Bridge.

*In 1935, he became a member of the Culbertson
organization as associate editor of* The Bridge World, *national sales manager for Kem cards, and one of Culbertson's regular teammates and partners.*

*He is the author of several books, the Editor-in-Chief
of the* Official Encyclopedia of Bridge, *Chairman of the
Goren Editorial Board, and has, for eleven years, served
as President of the International Bridge Press Association.
He was for nearly fifteen years, until his "retirement" in
1970, the Editor of the* Bulletin *of the American Contract
Bridge League, as well as director of public relations for
that organization—the largest in the world. He is present-
ly a consultant for the Precision Club, for which he edits
the bimonthly* Newsletter.

1. ROBERT HAMMAN (U.S.A.)

"If you are ever to amount to anything at this game, you must build up a picture of the unseen hands."

Robert Hamman is a name you will see repeatedly when you read reports of the really big events. Only 25 when he was runner-up in the 1964 Olympiad, he was a world team champion in 1970, 1971, and 1977, runner-up again in the 1972 Olympiad, and has represented North America on many other occasions, with many different partners. In 1974, he won the world Pairs Olympiad, playing with Bobby Wolff. He and Wolff now play for the professional team known as the Aces. Hammon is solidly built, a round-faced Rod Steiger.

In the first Bols Bridge Tip, Hamman went straight to the heart of things:

"Would you try to play golf or tennis blindfolded? That does not seem a very intelligent thing to do, but most players do exactly that when they play the hand at Contract Bridge.

"If you are ever to amount to anything at this game, you must build up a picture of the unseen hands. The idea is to know what the problem is before you try to solve it."

Early writers in the bridge tips competition were allowed less space than became normal later on, and

Hamman gave only one deal. Expanding his account, let us look first at the North-South hands only:

South dealer
Neither side vulnerable

North
♠ Q 5
♡ A 10 9 3 2
◇ 8 4
♣ 10 6 3 2

West
♡ 4 led

South
♠ A K 7 4 3 2
♡ 6
◇ Q 5
♣ A Q 8 4

South	West	North	East
1♠	2◇	Pass	Pass
2♠	Pass	3♠	Pass
4♠	Pass	Pass	Pass

North's raise to three spades is fairly close, I would say.

West led the 4 of hearts against Hamman's contract of four spades. It is instructive now to consider what you know—or need to assume—about each suit. Make a list of all the inferences that are available. Have you done that? It should read something like this:

First, spades. You haven't been doubled, so there is a good chance that they will be 3-2. In any case you must assume this, because you are surely going to lose two diamonds and at least one club. This is typical "assumption." Since the spades must be 3-2 if you are going to make the contract, you assume they *are* 3-2 and you build up your picture of the opposing hands on that basis.

Second, hearts. What do you make of that lead of the 4 of hearts? Could it be a singleton? Hardly, because that would give East K-Q-J-8-7-5 and he would have made a bid over two diamonds (especially since, as we shall see in a moment, he surely has a diamond honor). So West is leading low from an honor, or possibly two non-touching honors. He might have K-x-x, or Q-x-x, or K-J-x, something like that. Since he has bid diamonds and we are placing him with at least two spades, he is more likely to hold three hearts than four.

Third, diamonds. There is a simple, and very common, inference to be drawn here, but it is an inference often missed. With A-K of diamonds, West would surely have led this suit rather than a heart from some not very attractive holding. So the A-K of diamonds are split, with East probably clutching the King.

Fourth, clubs. Until we had studied the other suits, there wasn't much to say about the club situation. In fact, we have quite a lot of information. Since we are placing West with at least six diamonds, possibly seven, at least three hearts and at least two spades, he can hardly hold more than two clubs and may have only one. What about the King of clubs, a critical card? One pointer is that East is already marked with a high honor in hearts, quite possibly two honors, and with one of the top diamonds. Exaggerating a trifle, Hamman remarks: "East's silence would be incomprehensible with a diamond honor, at least one heart honor, and the King of clubs as well." There is another indication, at least as strong. West has chosen an unattractive lead in hearts, and there must be some reason why he preferred a heart to a club. Perhaps his club holding is a singleton King or K-x?

Now we are getting warm. Putting all the inferences together, we have arrived at the conclusion that the best way to limit the loss in clubs to one trick is to play West for short clubs, including the King. This is what Hamman did, with good effect, as can be seen from the full deal:

North
♠ Q 5
♡ A 10 9 3 2
♢ 8 4
♣ 10 6 3 2

West
♠ J 6
♡ K 5 4
♢ A J 10 9 6 3 2
♣ K

East
♠ 10 9 8
♡ Q J 8 7
♢ K 7
♣ J 9 7 5

South
♠ A K 7 4 3 2
♡ 6
♢ Q 5
♣ A Q 8 4

Having won the first trick with the Ace of hearts, the declarer played a club to the Ace, dropping the singleton King. There was still a little work to do, because the next club lead had to come from dummy. South had to hope that West held only two spades. He played Ace of spades and a spade to the Queen, then a low club from the table. East split his J-9-7, South played the Queen, and West was unable to ruff. The last trump was drawn, and declarer's 8 and 10 of clubs were now equals against East's Jack. This is how Hamman ended his account:

"Quickly I draw the last trump and concede a club

and two diamonds to make four spades. I notice only my partner is congratulating me. East is eyeing me suspiciously and West has already slid his chair a foot back from the table."

Before we leave this fine hand, let's just run over the inferences again, because if you think in this way every time you will soon be a champion:

Trumps had to be 3-2, because otherwise there would be no play for the contract.

The lead of the 4 of hearts was probably from K-x-x or Q-x-x, conceivably from K-J-x.

The Ace and King of diamonds were surely divided.

East was unlikely to hold the King of clubs for two reasons: with this card, he might have had enough to bid over his partner's two diamonds; and West's awkward lead in hearts pointed to an awkward holding in clubs as well, probably K-x or King alone.

This type of card-reading is the beginning, and almost the end, of all good play. The theme is present in almost all the contributions to this book. Instead of looking at other examples, therefore, it might be interesting to listen to Robert Hamman's opinions about a different feature of tournament play—the human side. One of the staff of the *ABTA Quarterly*, the magazine of American teachers, quizzed him about the perennial problem of the sort of welcome that novices get—or don't get—when they dip their toes in the tournament whirlpool.

Question: "Several of my pupils have gone out and

gotten into games and been scared to death by the attitude of the players. They hear criticism, partner against partner, even a player against the opponent, telling the opponent what he did wrong, and they get terribly upset about it. They won't go again."

Hamman: "Granted that there is substantial room for improvement in the demeanor of tournament players. Tournament bridge is a competitive event. It is competition, and in competition you do get a lot of tension and you get emotional reactions. It's not a sociable event in the sense of everybody get out and be friendly and kill some time. So as a bridge teacher you should condition them to the idea that this is a competitive event and this is competition, and it's great to solve problems and win, and that you're going to get a bit of static here and there; but you know, educate them to the fact that they will probably run into a situation like that sometime, but in reality nothing too bad has happened to them. If somebody turned to them and said 'Man, were you stupid,' well, chances are that someone just got a bad result. Now, would you rather get a good result and have your opponents say you're stupid, or get a bad result and have your opponents sit back with an inner smugness? So you can put it to them in that way: that usually the opponents are just blowing off steam and reacting to the fact that you did good and beat them.

"That will overcome some of it; now, it won't overcome all of it for all people. I think that a lot could be done toward conditioning people. The fact is that it is a competitive event and if something goes bad—if your partner does something incredibly stupid (naturally you yourself would never do anything incredibly stupid) and you get a terrible result—you're ready to lash out at anybody, heads must roll!"

To put it another way, if you take up boxing you must expect a few bloody noses.

2. RIXI MARKUS, M.B.E. (ENGLAND)

"When, as a defender, you are about to attack from a holding such as J-x, Q-x, or K-x, consider the possible advantage of leading a low card."

The second entry for the Bols competition was from Rixi Markus. I won't say she is the *best* woman player in the world, because bridge is a many-sided game that does not lend itself to individual comparisons, but she is certainly the most successful. She has won the women's pairs championship of the world twice and come second once. She has won the Mixed Team Olympiad, the Women's Team Olympiad, and six European titles. Incredibly, the first of these was gained for Austria back in 1935.

When I last saw her, as I was beginning to write this book, she was off to Abu Dhabi, then to Australia, and from there to California to visit the grave of her daughter, the beautiful film actress, Margo Lorenz, who died after a tragic illness. Quite a trip for a septuagenarian who recently had a skiing accident in Switzerland and could walk with difficulty; Rixi brings to life the same fierce intensity that uplifts her partners and daunts her opponents.

Rixi writes for the *Guardian* and the *Evening*

Standard, and is the author of several books, so let her speak for herself:

"When you, as a defender, are about to attack a suit in which you have a holding such as J-x, Q-x, or K-x, do you invariably lead the high card? Most players always do, but this is sometimes quite a costly mistake.

"My bridge tip is that when you have to open up such a holding, you should consider the possible advantage of leading the *low card*. This may well work better when the hand on your left is marked with strength in this suit, and especially when you have no re-entry to your hand.

"Suppose, for example, that at some point during the defense you lead the King from K-x and the next hand wins with the Ace from A-J-x. Now, if you yourself cannot regain the lead, your partner will be stymied—even if his holding is as strong as, say, Q-10-9-x. He will be unable to continue the suit except at the cost of a trick. Had you led low instead, the suit could have been cleared. (I am assuming, of course, that your partner is well endowed with entries.)

"I was able to put this tip to good use in a recent rubber. South opened with a weak 1NT, showing 12 to 14 points, and finished in 3NT after the sequence below. What would you have led from the West hand?

South dealer
Neither side vulnerable

North
♠ A K 10
♡ 6
♢ K J 9 8 5
♣ Q 7 4 2

West
♠ Q 2
♡ 10 7 4 3 2
♢ 6 4 3
♣ 8 6 5

East
♠ J 9 7 6 5 4
♡ A J 9
♢ A Q
♣ 10 3

South
♠ 8 3
♡ K Q 8 5
♢ 10 7 2
♣ A K J 9

The bidding:

South	West	North	East
1NT	Pass	2♣	2♠
Pass	Pass	Dble	Pass
3♡	Pass	3NT	Pass
Pass	Pass		

"As South was unwilling to pass his partner's penalty double of two spades, it seemed clear that the spade strength was likely to be in the dummy hand. Accordingly, in view of the absence of any re-entry to my own hand, I decided to lead the 2 of spades rather than the Queen.

"As you can see, declarer could no longer cope with his task. He won with the Ace, entered his hand with a club, and led a diamond, losing to my partner's Queen. Declarer ducked the spade return, allowing my Queen to hold, but I was able to put partner in with the Ace of hearts to clear the spades. Now South could take only eight tricks.

"It is easy to see that if West leads the Queen of spades initially, declarer will win with the Ace and make the contract, as East will be unable to attack spades effectively.

"These situations occur quite frequently during the middle game, when it often pays to lead a small card from a doubleton honor. This is especially so when you can see three or four cards smaller than your honor in dummy—provided that your partner is an intelligent player who can interpret the meaning of your plan of action."

In this last paragraph, Rixi is thinking of this type of situation:

North
962

West
AJ74

East
105

South
KQ83

East is on lead and the defense needs two tricks from this suit. If East has no further entry, he must lead the 5, not the 10, and West must read the situation: when he captures the Queen with the Ace he must steel himself to return the suit.

There is an excellent example of Rixi's Bols Bridge Tip in her book, *Aces and Places*, published by Secker & Warburg, involving the following hand:

East dealer
North-South vulnerable

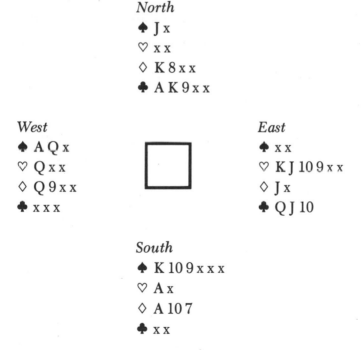

North
♠ J x
♡ x x
◇ K 8 x x
♣ A K 9 x x

West
♠ A Q x
♡ Q x x
◇ Q 9 x x
♣ x x x

East
♠ x x
♡ K J 10 9 x x
◇ J x
♣ Q J 10

South
♠ K 10 9 x x x
♡ A x
◇ A 10 7
♣ x x

Rixi writes: "I am very ambitious about defense. With a good partner you can try and beat contracts which seem unbeatable; but you need cooperation, which you get only from a first-class partner. Here it was Benito Garozzo who understood my reason for an unorthodox—but successful—attempt to beat four spades, which was made at every other table.

"After I had opened three hearts sitting East, South played in four spades and West led the Queen of hearts. I overtook with the King and declarer won with the Ace. He then crossed to dummy with a club and finessed a spade to Garozzo's Queen. I won the heart return, but what now? It seemed to me that with the clubs breaking even, I had to set up a diamond trick quickly, at the same time attacking dummy's entry. You will see that if I led the Jack of diamonds, West cannot continue the suit when in with the Ace of spades. So I had to find the lead of a low diamond."

There is another situation where it may be right to lead low from a doubleton honor, though with different intent. Imagine a suit divided as follows:

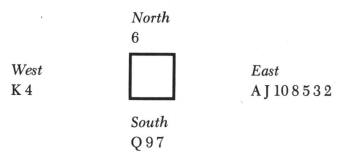

North
6

West
K 4

East
A J 10 8 5 3 2

South
Q 9 7

East has opened with a pre-empt in his long suit,

South has finished in 3NT, and West can tell, from the strength of his own hand, that his partner will have no side entry. If West leads the King the suit is dead; but if he leads low, and East puts in the 10, South will probably win the trick and communication will be established.

This is a variation of the same play:

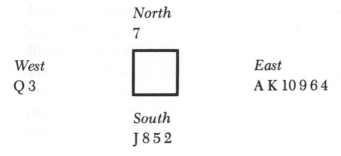

North
7

West
Q 3

East
A K 10 9 6 4

South
J 8 5 2

East has opened in third hand, the opponents have reached 3NT, and West has about 8 points. He can be sure there is little chance to establish and run his partner's suit after the normal lead of the Queen. He must lead the 3 and East must put in the 9 or 10, tempting South to win.

Quite often, the player in third position must make the critical play of low from a doubleton honor:

North
6 3

West
A 10 8 7 5 2

East
K J

South
Q 9 4

West leads the 7 and East can judge that his partner will have no quick entry. If East plays the King and follows with the Jack, South will duck and the suit will be dead. East must play the Jack, making it difficult for declarer to hold up the Queen.

Sometimes there is an opportunity for pretty combination between the defenders:

North dealer
Neither side vulnerable

North
♠ K 10 5
♡ A 4
◇ 10 6
♣ K J 10 8 5 2

West
♠ Q 3
♡ J 7
◇ J 9 7 5 4 2
♣ A 9 4

East
♠ 9 7 6 4 2
♡ Q 9 8 3
◇ A Q
♣ 6 3

South
♠ A J 8
♡ K 10 6 5 2
◇ K 8 3
♣ Q 7

South plays in 3NT after North has opened one club. West leads the 5 of diamonds. If East plays the

Ace and follows with the Queen, South will duck and the diamond suit will be shut out. East must put in the Queen of diamonds at trick one. Unless he can read the situation, South will win. Then East must be given a chance to dispose of his blocking Ace of diamonds on the third round of clubs.

3. GABRIEL CHAGAS (BRAZIL)

"When you have to develop a shaky suit, consider whether you can prepare for an intra-finesse by ducking with an 8 or a 9 on the first round."

Not easy, you might think, living and working in Brazil, to force yourself, in popular estimation, into the ranks of the top half-dozen players in the world; our third entrant, Gabriel Chagas, has done this in just a few years, playing mostly with Pedro Paulo Assumpção.

Chagas was 23 when he first appeared on the world bridge scene at Deauville, in the 1968 Team Olympiad. After representing Brazil in numerous Bermuda Bowls, he won the Team Olympiad at Monte Carlo in 1976 and followed this with outstanding performances in the annual event, the *Sunday Times Pairs*, winning by a big margin in 1979.

Gabriel holds a master's degree in actuarial mathematics. Fluent in Portuguese, Spanish, Italian, French, and English, familiar with German, Russian, and Japanese, and able to understand Swedish, Dutch, Hebrew, Hungarian, Tagalog (!), Arabic, Icelandic, and a few others, he must be by far the most cultivated bridge master in a linguistic sense; with his serious but friendly look, he is also one of the most popular.

His piece for the Bols competition is entitled "I Love Finesses:"

"The finesse is sometimes regarded as one of the humbler forms of play, but it sometimes requires quite a lot of imagination. This is especially true of the Intra-finesse—a play of which I am very fond. This diagram shows one common type of intra-finesse:

North
Q 8 5 3

West   *East*
J 7   K 10 4

South
A 9 6 2

"The bidding has given you quite a good idea of the layout of this suit. To hold yourself to one loser, you play small towards the dummy and finesse the 8! East will make the 10, but later you will enter the North hand and lead the Queen, pinning West's Jack. Well, this was an intra-finesse.

"Here's how an intra-finesse can arise in practical play:

North

♠ Q 9 2
♡ 6 5 4
◇ A Q 3
♣ K 8 4 3

West

♠ 10 6
♡ 10 9 8 2
◇ 5 4
♣ 10 9 7 5 2

East

♠ K J 7
♡ A K Q J
◇ 10 9 7 6
♣ Q J

South

♠ A 8 5 4 3
♡ 7 3
◇ K J 8 2
♣ A 6

"South plays in four spades after East has opened a strong notrump. West leads the 10 of hearts and South ruffs the third round. Knowing that East has the King of spades, South leads low to the 9, losing to the Jack.

"South wins the club return and takes a second and third round of this suit to test the distribution. With East showing out, South decides to place him with three trumps. So, after ruffing the third club, he crosses with a diamond and leads the Queen of spades.

"A veteran intra-finesser now, you find yourself in four hearts on the next deal after a club overcall by West.

North
♠ K J 2
♡ A 9 2
◇ K 9 6 2
♣ 9 6 3

West
♠ 8 6
♡ J 5
◇ Q 10 3
♣ K Q J 10 8 7

East
♠ 10 9 7 5 4
♡ Q 10 7 6
◇ 8 4
♣ 5 4

South
♠ A Q 3
♡ K 8 4 3
◇ A J 7 5
♣ A 2

"You duck the first club and West continues the suit. As a 3-3 trump break is unlikely, you lead a low heart towards the dummy, and when West follows with the 5 you finesse the 9!

"East wins with the 10 and switches to a spade, confirming that the clubs are 6-2. You cash the trump Ace, and when this collects the Jack from West, you pick up East's remaining trumps by finessing the 8.

"On the fourth trump you throw, not a club, but a diamond from dummy. The successful intra-finesse has brought you to nine tricks, but now you must establish a diamond for game.

"As you are wide open in clubs you lead a low diamond, intending to finesse the 9 into East's hand. West, however, inserts the 10. You win with dummy's King and cash the remaining spades. When West shows out on the third spade, you have a perfect count. West began with six clubs, two hearts, and two spades—and therefore three diamonds.

"You need no more finesses. On the third spade, West is forced down to two diamonds and the Jack of clubs. You therefore lead dummy's losing club, throwing West in and forcing him to lead into your diamond tenace.

"This ending was very satisfying—but you would never have got there without the aid of the intra-finesse in the trump suit.

"My bridge tip, therefore, is that whenever you have to develop a shaky suit, and especially when this suit is trump, you should consider whether you can prepare for an intra-finesse by ducking with an 8 or a 9 on the first round.

"Happy finessing!"

There are many variations of this theme. Most players know what to do with this combination:

J 9
A 8 7 5 4 2

The only chance to hold the losers to one is to lead low and finesse the 9 (unless West plays an honor). If this loses to the King or Queen, your next play is the

Jack from dummy, pinning the 10 if West started with 10-x.

When two intermediate cards are missing, you can achieve surprising results when both are favorably placed:

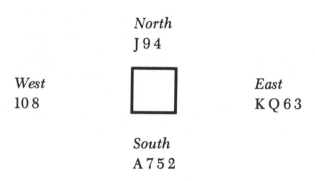

North
J 9 4

West
10 8

East
K Q 6 3

South
A 7 5 2

You lead low from hand, covering West's 8 with the 9 and losing to the King or Queen. On the next round, you lead the Jack, pinning the 10, and you still hold the major tenace, 7-5 over East's 6-3. It may be noted that in many of these situations, it is good deceptive play for the second hand to play his higher card on the first round, just as it is usually correct to play the Jack from J-9.

There is a different type of intra-finesse (Chagas's description has passed into the language) that is very seldom mentioned in bridge literature. Consider this deal:

West dealer
North-South vulnerable

North
♠ 8 4
♡ 9 3
♦ 9 7 6 4 3
♣ A 10 9 7

West
♠ Q 9 7 3
♡ Q 10 8 6 4 2
♦ 5 2
♣ 4

East
♠ J 5
♡ A J 5
♦ K J 10 8
♣ Q 6 5 3

South
♠ A K 10 6 2
♡ K 7
♦ A Q
♣ K J 8 2

South	West	North	East
—	Pass	Pass	1 ♦
Dble	1 ♡	Pass	Pass
2NT	Pass	3NT	Pass
Pass	Pass		

Spurning his partner's suit, West leads the 6 of hearts. East wins and returns a heart.

Assuming that the diamond finesse will be right,

South needs to make four tricks in clubs. Because of the entry situation, he must lead the Jack of clubs—no other card. Having overtaken the Jack with the Ace, he leads the 10, unblocking with the 8. Then he can make four club tricks and still be in dummy for the diamond finesse.

Someone showed me recently an extremely difficult hand with the same theme:

South dealer
North-South vulnerable

North
♠ Q
♡ A 10 9 4 3
♢ 9 8 7
♣ K J 6 2

West
♠ A J 10 9 7 6 5 3
♡ K J 8 5
♢ —
♣ 7

East
♠ 4 2
♡ Q 7 2
♢ K 10 6 4
♣ Q 10 5 4

South
♠ K 8
♡ 6
♢ A Q J 5 3 2
♣ A 9 8 3

West is a cunning fellow and the bidding goes:

South	West	North	East
1♦	1♠	2♡	Pass
3♦	4♠	5♦	Dble
Pass	Pass	Pass	

West begins with Ace and another spade. How can South make his contract of five diamonds doubled? Even with a sight of all the cards, you might battle at this for hours without striking the right answer.

Everything hangs on the pips in clubs. South wins the second spade in hand, discarding a heart from dummy and noting East's echo. If West holds two clubs, or the singleton 10 or Queen, the contract is laydown, because declarer can pick up the trumps without loss and make three tricks in clubs.

The critical situation is when West has the singleton 7 of clubs. Preparing for this, South leads the 8 of clubs at trick three. Seeing West's 7, he plays low from dummy. East wins with the 10 and exits with a heart to dummy's Ace.

Declarer now plays diamonds until East covers. South wins and leads the 9 of clubs to dummy's King. Now, with J-6 of clubs in dummy, A-3 in hand, he can pick up East's Q-5 and still be in a position to finesse again in diamonds.

4. TERENCE REESE (ENGLAND)

"Study the early discards and consider this point: From what holding would the defender most readily have made those discards?"

Introducing my entry for the Bols competition, the old flatterer, Albert Dormer, wrote in the *IBPA Bulletin:*

"IBPA members would rightly feel irked if regaled with an account of Terence Reese's contributions to theory, his widely admired books, and his achievements as a player. His working life has been almost entirely devoted to bridge, and indeed the late Guy Ramsey, an IBPA President, wrote in his classic book, *Aces All,* '...an almost pre-natal influence towards cards wrought its influence upon him. His parents met when they were introduced to one another as First Lady and First Gentleman at a whist drive.'"

The rest of the gory details are in my autobiographical *Bridge at the Top.* For those interested in later developments, I seem now to have written about 50 books on bridge, poker, canasta, backgammon, and casino gambling, plus a novel of searing passion, *Trick Thirteen,* with Jeremy Flint. In recent years, I have become, to my heavy cost, a backgammon addict.

In my bridge tip, I advised the declarer to study the early discards and consider this point: From what opening would the defender most readily have made those discards?

The answer will often resolve a critical guess. For example, a defender who holds A-5-3-2 or K-5-3-2 will discard from that suit more readily than if he had held Q-5-3-2 or J-5-3-2. That will give you a clue in situations of this kind:

(1)

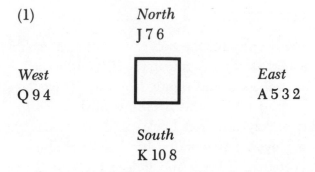

North
J 7 6

West
Q 9 4

East
A 5 3 2

South
K 10 8

This is a side suit in a trump contract and declarer needs to establish one fast trick. East has made two early discards, the 2 and the 3. Conclusion: he is more likely to hold A-x-x-x than Q-x-x-x.

(2)

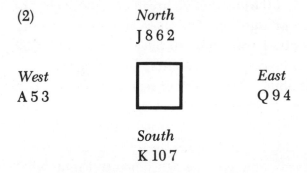

North
J 8 6 2

West
A 5 3

East
Q 9 4

South
K 10 7

This time West discards the 3 before he is under any great pressure. Conclusion: he is more likely to have discarded from A-x-x than from Q-x-x.

(3)

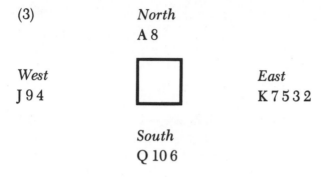

North
A 8

West
J 9 4

East
K 7 5 3 2

South
Q 10 6

With no particular sign of regret, East parts with the 2 and the 3 at an early stage. When you play the Ace and 8, he follows with the 5 and 7. Play him for K-x-x-x-x rather than J-x-x-x-x.

(4)

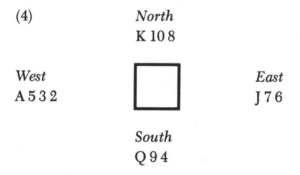

North
K 10 8

West
A 5 3 2

East
J 7 6

South
Q 9 4

West discards twice. He is more likely to have come down to A-x than to J-x; but if a low card to the King is headed by the Ace, be inclined to play East for A-J-x (because West, with J-x-x-x, would not have unguarded the Jack until he had to).

Such inferences are especially strong when dummy has what may seem to a defender to be an establishable suit, as here:

South dealer
Neither side vulnerable

North
♠ 10 5 2
♡ K J 6 3
◇ A 7 3
♣ 8 6 4

West
♠ 9 3
♡ Q 10 8
◇ 10 9 5 4
♣ K J 7 3

East
♠ J 7
♡ A 9 5 2
◇ J 8 6
♣ A 10 9 5

South
♠ A K Q 8 6 4
♡ 7 4
◇ K Q 2
♣ Q 2

South	West	North	East
1♠	Pass	1NT	Pass
3♠	Pass	4♠	Pass
Pass	Pass		

West leads the 3 of clubs and South ruffs the third round. There is something to be said for leading a heart at once, putting West under some pressure if he holds the Ace, but instead, the declarer plays four rounds of trumps, discarding a diamond from dummy. (It is good play to keep the heart holding intact.) West throws a club and a diamond, East a club and a heart.

After cashing three diamonds, South leads a heart; West plays the 8. South should finesse the Jack. Why? Because of East's heart discard. With A-9-x-x East, expecting the contract to depend on the heart guess, would not think it necessary to keep all four. But with Q-9-x-x, he would not let go a heart, in case declarer held A-x and might attempt to establish the suit by ruffing the third round.

As so often, the discard tells the story.

The early discards will often give a clue to length, as well as to the position of honor cards. This is a common example:

A K 7 3
Q 5

Defending against a notrump contract, East, at his first opportunity, discards from the suit shown. You may be sure that he did not begin with four of the suit; possibly three, more likely five; and if he discards twice, then the odds are that he began with six, and you can count his partner for a singleton.

There are, of course, chances for a clever defender to mislead. I tackled this problem in a follow-up article, entitled *The Other Side of the Coin:*

"There are two sides to every question, it is said, and certainly there are two sides to my Bols Tip, 'Watch the early discards.' The defenders should aim to avoid making discards that reveal their distribution. Suppose this hand is played in a match between two teams:

South dealer
Both sides vulnerable

North
♠ K Q 8 4
♡ 8 5 2
◇ A 5 3
♣ K 7 6

West
♠ J 7 5
♡ K J 9 4
◇ 1 0 8 4 2
♣ Q 5

East
♠ 1 0 9 6 3 2
♡ A 7 6
◇ Q 9 6
♣ 1 0 9

South
♠ A
♡ Q 1 0 3
◇ K J 7
♣ A J 8 4 3 2

The bidding goes:

South	West	North	East
1♣	Pass	1♠	Pass
2♣	Pass	3♣	Pass
3NT	Pass	Pass	Pass

"The defenders begin with four rounds of hearts. At the first table, dummy throws a club on the fourth heart, East a spade, and South a club. West switches to a diamond, the Queen losing to the King.

"South, a Bols man, cashes the Ace of spades, takes two more diamonds and the K-Q of spades. By this time, East has shown up with three hearts and three diamonds, and the clear inference from his discard of a spade at trick four is that he began with five spades. No reason, therefore, to place East with more than two clubs. Declarer plays for the drop and makes his contract.

"At the second table East also is a Bols man. Judging that the contract will easily be made unless South can be induced to take a losing finesse in clubs, he plans from the first to create the impression that he holds length in clubs. At trick four, instead of the obvious— but revealing—spade, he throws a diamond. Playing the cards in the same order as before, South arrives at this end position:

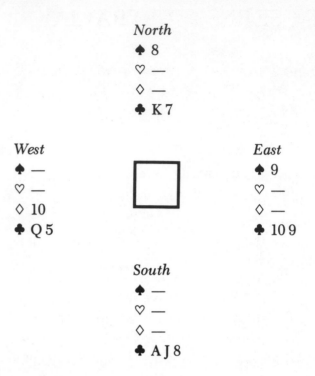

North

♠ 8
♡ —
◇ —
♣ K 7

West

♠ —
♡ —
◇ 10
♣ Q 5

East

♠ 9
♡ —
◇ —
♣ 10 9

South

♠ —
♡ —
◇ —
♣ A J 8

"Reflecting that East did not throw a spade until he had to find a discard on the third round of diamonds, declarer counts him for 4-3-3-3 distribution and takes the club finesse. Unlucky! Down two."

5. TIM SERES (AUSTRALIA)

"When you can see that declarer is bound to succeed by normal play, look for a chance to give him a losing option."

Tim Seres left war-torn Hungary as a youth, emigrating to Sydney, Australia. The Hungarians have always been a nation of great card-players and Seres was soon recognized as the outstanding bridge player in a continent isolated from the world's top performers. His first impact on the wider scene was made when he visited Europe in the late '50s, cutting a swathe in the ranks of money players at London's Hamilton Club.

By force of example, and his own exceptional skill, Seres carried his country to the front rank. Australia came 6th out of 29 in the 1964 Team Olympiad and 3rd in the 1971 Bermuda Bowl, ahead of Brazil and the U.S.A. In 1968, Australia missed an Olympiad semi-final berth by only 7 victory points, behind Canada's score of 451.

In recent years, Australia's performance has been relatively disappointing. Amid wrangles over team selection, training and captaincy, many sigh for the days when Tim was given a more or less free hand in this area. Greater Trust Hath No Man . . .

Modest, urbane, and soft-spoken, Seres has the comfortable air of a business chief. His hobby is horse-racing; more than a hobby, for it is said that by bringing his skill and judgment to bear on this sport, he has made a fortune.

The theme of his tip is "Give Declarer Enough Rope:"

"In the long haul, you win at bridge by avoiding error rather than by being brilliant. The expert may display an occasional glimpse of genius or elegance, but he owes his preeminence to the fact that he makes fewer mistakes than his fellow players.

"Because bridge is a game of errors, you should try to develop the knack of giving an opponent the chance to go wrong. One way of doing this is by providing the declarer with a choice of plays in a situation where he would otherwise be bound to make the winning play. Most tournament players will be familiar with this situation:

North
A Q 10 3

West   *East*
J 9 7 5   4

South
K 8 6 2

"This is the trump suit and declarer starts by laying down dummy's Ace. If West follows small, declarer will play low to the King on the next round, exposing the finesse against the Jack. (Declarer has no way to succeed if East has J-9-x-x.) West, however, should drop the 9 on the first round. Now declarer may continue with dummy's Queen, playing East for J-x-x-x.

"The next example is also fairly well known:

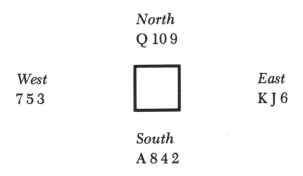

North
Q 10 9

West
7 5 3

East
K J 6

South
A 8 4 2

"South plays low to the 10. If East wins with the Jack, declarer has no choice but to enter dummy and finesse against the King on the next round. East therefore should win the first trick with the King. This affords declarer a losing option, as he may finesse the 9 on the next round, playing West for J-x-x-x.

"Opportunities for such plays come along much more frequently than players realize. The following deal occurred in a top-class pairs event:

South dealer
Both sides vulnerable

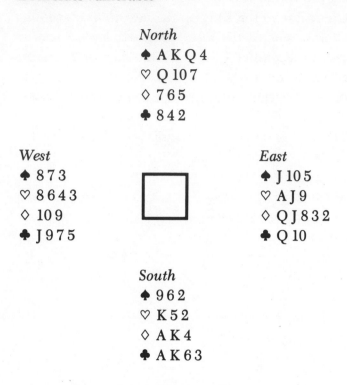

North
- ♠ A K Q 4
- ♡ Q 10 7
- ◊ 7 6 5
- ♣ 8 4 2

West
- ♠ 8 7 3
- ♡ 8 6 4 3
- ◊ 10 9
- ♣ J 9 7 5

East
- ♠ J 10 5
- ♡ A J 9
- ◊ Q J 8 3 2
- ♣ Q 10

South
- ♠ 9 6 2
- ♡ K 5 2
- ◊ A K 4
- ♣ A K 6 3

"Whether South opened 1NT or one club, he was likely to finish in 3NT. West usually led the 10 of diamonds, hoping to hit his partner's suit. All declarers but one succeeded easily, making four spade tricks, two diamonds, two clubs, and a heart. How could a top declarer fail?

"At this table, South won the diamond lead and tested spades. On the Ace and King of this suit, East dropped the Jack and 10! Not surprisingly, declarer assumed that the spades were 4-2 and continued by playing low to the 9, hoping to reenter dummy with a heart. But East, of course, ducked the King of hearts when this was led. The contract could have been made by an end-play (cash second diamond and two top clubs, then exit with a diamond), but South staked his fortunes on a finesse of the 10 of hearts and so finished a trick short.

"The hapless declarer had fallen victim to a defender who followed the very profitable adage, "Give declarer enough rope . . ."

"My bridge tip, therefore, is just this: when you can see that declarer is bound to succeed by normal play, look for a chance to give him a losing option.

"It stands to reason that if you consistently give your opponent a chance to go wrong, he will sometimes take it!"

An interesting gloss can be added to Seres' first example. Imagine that you are playing a slam contract with one of these trump combinations:

(1)   K 8 4 2   (2)   K Q 10 3
      A Q 10 3   A 8 7 2

With (1) you are naturally going to play first one of the honors from your own hand, and it may not seem to matter whether you lay down the Ace or lead from dummy toward the Ace. But by leading the Ace first, you are laying a small trap for yourself. East, with J-9-x-x, will see that his hand is dead if he plays low, so he will contribute the 9. (Tournament players know this position quite well.) Then you will have to guess the continuation. But if you lead from dummy on the first round, it will be dangerous for East to play the 9 from J-9-x-x, because partner might hold the singleton 10, giving the defense a certain trick. Similarly, with the cards as in (2), it is best to lead low from hand. If, instead, you lead the King, and East follows with a low card, West, with J-9-x-x, may make the deceptive play, giving you a guess.

The play of the 9 from J-9-x-x belongs to the extensive tribe of "obligatory false cards." These are well-known examples:

(3)   *North*
           J 5 4

West   [ ]   *East*
10 9 3   K 7

         South
         A Q 8 6 2

(4)   *North*
           7

West   [ ]   *East*
J 10 6   A 4

         South
         K Q 9 8 5 3 2

In (3), when declarer finesses the Queen, West must drop the 9 or 10, so that declarer will have the option of leading the Jack on the next round. In (4) the 7 is led to the Queen; West must drop the Jack or 10, leaving the declarer with alternative plays.

The second example given by Seres (where East plays the King from K-J-x) has some attractive variations:

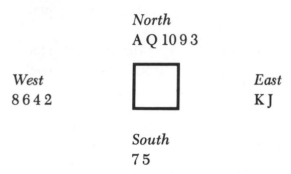

North
A Q 10 9 3

West
8 6 4 2

East
K J

South
7 5

Suppose that declarer has reason to place East with the King. He may well begin by finessing the 9. To win with the King now is essential. If you win with the Jack, South will go up with the Ace on the next round; but if you head the 9 with the King, he will finesse the 10 on the next round and you will make two tricks.

In the full deal described by Seres, the declarer is misled because a defender drops the J-10 of spades under dummy's A-K. It may be said, first, that in good company, the declarer should not be diverted by this play. There are innumerable situations where a defender may gain by dropping a card that will inevitably appear on the next round.

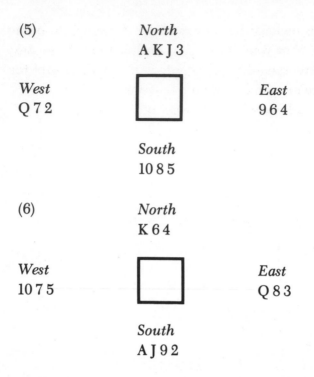

(5)   **North**
              A K J 3

West   **East**
Q 7 2   9 6 4

              South
              10 8 5

(6)   **North**
              K 6 4

West   **East**
10 7 5   Q 8 3

              South
              A J 9 2

In (5) South leads low and finesses the Jack successfully. When the Ace follows, West should try the effect of dropping the Queen. Declarer may then waste an entry by crossing to the 10. Example (6) is slightly different. When the declarer, at notrumps, leads the King from dummy and follows with a low card, East (unless there is a danger that South may hold five cards) should insert the Queen. This may well cause the declarer to conclude that the suit is breaking 4-2; he may refrain from cashing the Jack, and may even attempt an end-play against West's imagined 10-8.

In each of these last two examples, the play of the

Queen is in accordance with the principle of dropping the card that you will be known to hold after the next trick. Observe how the seemingly innocent play of the 9 can create havoc in these two positions:

(7)

	North K 10 8 4 2	
West Q J 6 5	☐	*East* 9 3
	South A 7	

(8)

	North A 5	
West K 9 3	☐	*East* J 7 6
	South Q 10 8 4 2	

In (7) the declarer, seeking to establish four tricks at notrumps, leads the Ace. If East plays low, South will put in dummy's 10 on the next round; but if East drops the 9 under the Ace, declarer will have the option of playing him for Q-9 or J-9, and may play the King on the second round.

In (8) the suit shown is the trump suit. Declarer

plays the Ace from dummy and then leads toward the Q-10-8-4. Again the 9 from West on the first trick may cause a misplay. If the 9 has been played, South may go up with the Queen, winning four tricks when West has J-9 alone; but if West plays the 3, declarer's natural card on the second round is the 10.

6. GIORGIO BELLADONNA (ITALY)

"When, as a defender, you hold the Ace of trumps, consider whether to hold up this card when trumps are first played."

Belladonna stands, with Garozzo, at the top of the list of the world's most successful players. He has won the world team championship, either Bermuda Bowl or Olympiad, a mind-boggling 17 times!

I remember quite well the impression I received during the 1958 world championship at Como between Italy and North America. It was the first time bridgerama had been used in an international match. Belladonna and Avarelli played almost all the time in the closed room. Whenever the Americans on bridgerama missed their way on a difficult bidding hand, they were invariably punished. Belladonna and Avarelli, playing the Roman Club, were devastating.

Giorgio is fond of music and a keen photographer. He has the sort of rumbustious bonhomie that Italian film-makers like to attach to popular priests; no wonder he has a very successful bridge club in Rome. Playing against him at the table, you are conscious of his eyes. I say this in no derogatory sense. His eyes flicker from side to side, like a fly darting from place to place on a wall. You feel they reflect an inquiring mind, searching for the solution to a tricky problem; and, by God, he always finds it.

Giorgio's tip is entitled "Hold Up the Ace of Trumps:"

"The most powerful card in bridge is the Ace of trumps. When you, as a defender, are fortunate enough to hold this card, you must be sure to put it to the best possible use.

"A general does not necessarily commit his crack troops to the battle right at the start, and you too should quite often hold back the Ace of trumps until it can play a decisive role. In this deal you are West:

West dealer
Neither side vulnerable

North
♠ 10 9 6
♡ 10 3 2
◇ A Q J 5
♣ A K 2

West
♠ A 7 4 2
♡ K Q J 8 6
◇ 9
♣ Q 10 5

East
♠ 5 3
♡ 9 7 4
◇ 10 6 4 3 2
♣ J 8 7

South
♠ K Q J 8
♡ A 5
◇ K 8 7
♣ 9 6 4 3

South	West	North	East
—	1♡	Pass	Pass
Dble	Pass	2♡	Pass
2♠	Pass	3♠	Pass
4♠	Pass	Pass	Pass

"You lead the King of hearts and South wins with the Ace. If South can force out the Ace of trumps, he will have 10 easy tricks. A resourceful declarer will not lead trumps from his own hand, for this would make it plain that he had a strong sequence. South is likely, instead, to cross to dummy with a club or diamond and lead a low spade to the King.

"Suppose that you release the Ace. In this case, the contract will be made. You can cash the Queen of hearts and continue with the Jack, but South simply discards a losing club. Now he can win any continuation, draw trumps, and claim the contract.

"Now suppose, instead, that you hold up the Ace of trumps on the first round. Declarer continues with a second trump, but you duck this also. South is now helpless. If he plays a third trump, you win and play hearts, forcing South to ruff with his last trump. In this case, you beat the contract by two tricks. If South abandons trumps after two rounds, you eventually make your small trump by ruffing, and South winds up with nine tricks.

"It is not only when you are long in trumps that you should be reluctant to part with the Ace. In the next deal, you are East.

South dealer
East-West vulnerable

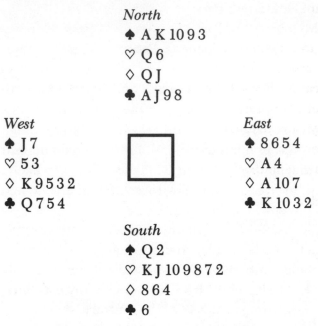

North
♠ A K 10 9 3
♡ Q 6
◊ Q J
♣ A J 9 8

West
♠ J 7
♡ 5 3
◊ K 9 5 3 2
♣ Q 7 5 4

East
♠ 8 6 5 4
♡ A 4
◊ A 10 7
♣ K 10 3 2

South
♠ Q 2
♡ K J 10 9 8 7 2
◊ 8 6 4
♣ 6

"South opens three hearts and North raises to four hearts. West leads the 3 of diamonds and you win with the Ace.

"As the 3 of diamonds is presumably your partner's fourth-best, you can place South with three diamonds. The opening pre-empt suggests a seven-card suit, so South can have only three cards in the black suits—all taken care of by dummy's Ace-King of spades and Ace of clubs. Unless you can take three diamond tricks, you are unlikely to beat four hearts.

"If you were to return the Ace and another trump, with the object of preventing a diamond ruff, South would easily take the balance. To keep control, you must hold on to the Ace of trumps and return a *low* trump. Now South must go down.

"My Bols bridge tip, therefore, is simple: whenever you, as a defender, include the Ace of trumps among your assets, you should consider whether to hold up this card when trumps are first played. After all, the Ace of trumps is the one card in the pack that you are always sure to make!"

Sometimes it is necessary to hold up for two rounds when you hold only A-x-x:

East dealer
Both sides vulnerable

North
♠ K 7
♡ 9 5 2
◇ Q 10 7 4
♣ J 7 5 2

West
♠ J 9 5
♡ A 6 4
◇ 9 6 3
♣ K Q 10 3

East
♠ 10 8 6 4 2
♡ 8 7 3
◇ J 5
♣ A 8 4

South
♠ A Q 3
♡ K Q J 10
◇ A K 8 2
♣ 9 6

South	West	North	East
—	—	—	Pass
1♡	Pass	2♡	Pass
3◇	Pass	3♡	Pass
4♡	Pass	Pass	Pass

South plays in four hearts and West leads the King of clubs, followed by a low club to the Ace. East plays a third club, which South, having three top losers, is obliged to ruff.

Declarer may cross to the King of spades and lead a low heart to the King, in an attempt to dislodge the Ace. It is clear that if West wins the first— or even the second—round of trumps, South will easily succeed. He will ruff a fourth round of clubs, enter dummy with a diamond, and draw the outstanding trumps with the 9.

But observe the effect of holding up twice: South cannot play a third round, because then West will win and cash the Queen of clubs, and if instead South plays on diamonds, East will ruff the third round with a low trump.

Pursuing the same theme, a defender who holds A-K-x of the trump suit (or A-Q-x over the King) may have a chance to embarrass the declarer.

North dealer
Neither side vulnerable

North
♠ 8 4 2
♡ A Q J
◇ 7 4 3
♣ K Q 6 5

West
♠ A K 3
♡ 9 6 4
◇ K Q J 8
♣ 10 7 2

East
♠ J 5
♡ K 8 7 3
◇ A 9 6 5 2
♣ 9 3

South
♠ Q 10 9 7 6
♡ 10 5 2
◇ 10
♣ A J 8 4

South	West	North	East
—	—	Pass	Pass
Pass	1◇	Dble	3◇
3♠	Pass	Pass	Pass

The defenders begin with two rounds of diamonds, South ruffing. A heart finesse loses to the King and South is punched again in diamonds. After a heart to the Ace, the position is:

North
♠ 8 4 2
♡ J
♢ —
♣ K Q 6 5

West
♠ A K 3
♡ 9
♢ 8
♣ 10 7 2

East
♠ J 5
♡ 8 3
♢ A 9
♣ 9 3

South
♠ Q 10 9
♡ 10
♢ —
♣ A J 8 4

Declarer leads a low spade from dummy and finesses the 10. A player in West's position might think he would be losing a tempo if he held off, but that is not the case at all. If West wins, there is no defense. But if West holds off, South is in the same kind of dilemma as on the previous deal. He cannot afford to play another round of trumps—and he cannot afford not to!

7. BOBBY WOLFF (U.S.A.)

"Do not be content simply to work out the high cards a defender is likely to hold: try to assess his distribution as well."

Bobby Wolff was a founder-member of the team known as the Dallas Aces, which was formed in 1968. In those days, his reputation was greater, perhaps, among his fellow-experts than among the bridge public, but he soon hit the headlines. Playing first with Jim Jacoby, later with Robert Hamman, he won the world championship in 1970, 1971, and 1977, was three times runner-up, and runner-up also in the Teams Olympiad. He won the Mixed Teams Olympiad at Miami in 1972, and the World Pairs in 1974. He is the only player in bridge history to have won all three titles: Pairs, Teams, and Mixed Teams.

Short and rotund, quiet but authoritative, Wolff is the only player to have stayed with the Aces throughout. It says much, both for his loyalty and his flexibility. In recent years, he has often been director of the bidding panel of the *Bridge World*. Many times I have been impressed by the wit and wisdom of his observations.

Wolff's tip, on the theme of discovery, is entitled "Check Out the Distribution."

"Some of the clues concerning the unseen hands are rather obvious: an opponent who has opened the bidding is likely to have at least 13 points, and so on and so forth.

"Obvious—but not entirely reliable. The successful declarer does not rest content with these easy clues, but tries to unearth additional information. This challenging hand from match play shows the process at work:

East dealer
Both sides vulnerable

North
♠ 9 8 7 5
♡ A J 8 3
♢ K Q 7
♣ 8 2

West
♣ 5 led

South
♠ A Q 10 6 3
♡ 5
♢ 9 3
♣ K Q J 10 7

The bidding went:

South	West	North	East
—	—	—	1♣
1♠	2♦	4♠	Pass
Pass	Pass		

"The spade game was reached at both tables in a team-of-four match, and the play to each trick was identical. However, one declarer based his play on flimsy reasoning, while the other had a sure bet.

"West led the 5 of clubs and East took the Ace, shifting to the 2 of diamonds. West won with the Ace and returned a diamond, ruffed by East, who exited with a club. This trick was won by declarer as West followed suit.

"The defenders had taken three tricks and South had to pick up the spade suit without loss. Both declarers crossed to dummy's Ace of hearts and led the 9 of spades, on which East played low. How should South play to this trick?"

This may be the moment to interrupt Bobby Wolff's account. See how close you can come to an analysis of the distribution. How much do you know so far? Diamonds 7-1, clubs presumably 4-2; is there anything you can add to that? Wolff continued:

"Both declarers played low on the spade lead. The 9 held the trick, and now another spade took care of the trumps, allowing the game to be scored. The full hand was:

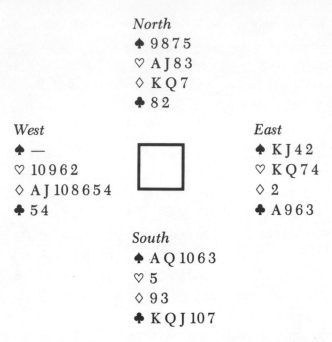

North
♠ 9 8 7 5
♡ A J 8 3
◇ K Q 7
♣ 8 2

West
♠ —
♡ 10 9 6 2
◇ A J 10 8 6 5 4
♣ 5 4

East
♠ K J 4 2
♡ K Q 7 4
◇ 2
♣ A 9 6 3

South
♠ A Q 10 6 3
♡ 5
◇ 9 3
♣ K Q J 10 7

"The first declarer remarked: 'I played for the double finesse in spades because East had opened. West had shown up with five points and I reckoned that East needed both spade honors for his bid.'

"A good reason. But is it good enough? Suppose East had not held the Jack of spades. Might he not have opened the bidding just the same? The singleton diamond surely would have persuaded him, so declarer did not really have valid grounds for the deep finesse.

"Why did the second declarer play West for a void in spades? The answer is hidden in both the bidding and the play. East, who had opened one club, had shown up with only four cards in this suit. He therefore could not have had five cards in either hearts or spades, and as he had a singleton diamond, he must be precisely 4-4-1-4. So West had to be void in spades."

Wolff's tip, therefore, was that you should not be content simply to work out the high cards a defender is likely to have for the bids he has made. You must also try to picture his distribution, for this may provide you with an even surer guide to the winning play.

Nothing is certain, it used to be said, except death and taxes; to which, in the present world, one must add industrial disputes. For bridge players, an equally safe proposition is that there are 52 cards in the pack and that each player began with 13. In that simple fact, as Bobby Wolff points out, lies most of the skill in this game. Two deals follow that illustrate his theme.

North dealer
Neither side vulnerable

North
♠ Q J 2
♡ K J 9 5
◊ K 7 3
♣ 9 7 6

West
♣ K led

South
♠ A K 10 9 3
♡ A 4 3
◊ A 6
♣ Q 4 2

The bidding goes:

South	West	North	East
—	—	Pass	Pass
1♠	2♣	2♠	Pass
3♠	Pass	4♠	Pass
Pass	Pass		

The defense begins with three rounds of clubs, East discarding a heart on the second round and ruffing the third. He exits with a trump and the declarer draws three rounds, East (who has ruffed once) discarding two diamonds.

Most players would take the heart finesse now, but that's not right. The correct technique is to play three rounds of diamonds, the object being to gain more information about the defending hands. As it turns out, both opponents follow to three rounds of diamonds.

You know now that West began with six clubs, three spades, and three diamonds. So the normal finesse against the Queen of hearts cannot work. West has a singleton heart, and it may be the 10. So the next play is a low heart to the King.

As the last deal showed, it is often incorrect to play the critical suit first. A little information in other departments may tell you *how* to play the critical suit.

North dealer
Both sides vulnerable

North
♠ A 9 6
♡ A K 9 4
◇ A Q
♣ K 10 5 2

West	*East*
♠ 10 7 3	♠ 8 5 4 2
♡ 8 6 3	♡ Q 10 5
◇ J 10 9 5 4 2	◇ 7 3
♣ 8	♣ Q 9 6 3

South
♠ K Q J
♡ J 7 2
◇ K 8 6
♣ A J 7 4

North opened one club; and South, as players will, responded 3NT. (This call might have led to a silly result if North had been short in hearts; a mark-time bid of one diamond would have been a better reply.) Over 3 NT, North had an obvious raise to 6NT.

West led the Jack of diamonds, and the declarer's first move was to enter his hand with the King of spades and finesse in clubs—the wrong way. Eventually, he had to lose a heart as well.

The early club finesse toward East was wrong for two reasons. First, if West has the singleton 8 or 9 of clubs, it is possible to develop four tricks in the suit, so the King should be led first. Secondly, there can be no harm in fishing around for information. The Ace and King of hearts should be played off, and, as it happens, the 10 falls on the second round, making it safe to play a third round. In due course, South discovers that West had six diamonds, three spades and three hearts. A club finesse through East becomes a certainty, and three club tricks are enough for the slam.

8. CHARLES GOREN (U.S.A.)

"As a defender, consider the advantage of ducking to conceal the lie of the cards or to spoil the timing for a squeeze."

Charles Goren's Bols Tip was introduced in the *IBPA Bulletin* with a certain degree of awe: "Charles Goren, one of a handful of IBPA Honor members, was invited to join the Bols competition *honoris causa* (as an honor) as a token of his fellow-members' esteem for his work in popularizing bridge and in recognition of his pre-eminence in teaching bridge via the written word."

The tribute was well deserved. A lawyer by profession, Goren began to play tournament bridge in 1931. At the end of the war, and just after, in the days when competition was not so fierce as it is now, he accumulated a vast total of master points. He promptly seized the opportunity to occupy the vacuum that had been created by Culbertson's loss of drive. His books were always clear and well written, but oddly enough, he contributed very little to theory. The early Goren was almost indistinguishable in effect from Culbertson, retaining all the bad features such as the Forcing Two opening with a 2NT response. His adoption of the distributional point count, however, was a move of far-reaching importance, for it enabled quite untalented players to attain a degree of competence. Also, over the years, Goren accepted—with much better grace than Culbertson—the good ideas of other players.

Just as there was a pretense among the knowing ones that Josephine was a better player than Ely, so it was often said by rivals that Goren owed most of his tournament success to his partner, Helen Sobel. Helen was undoubtedly a great player, but I saw enough of Goren's play in British tournaments and in the 1956 world championship in Paris to establish that he was a top-class performer by any standards.

Even at that time, Goren—though humorous, friendly, and unassuming—showed signs of the nervous strain that is often the precursor of failing health. He now lives quietly in Miami. His substantial travel and publishing interests under the Goren International umbrella were administered for many years by the late Harold Ogust, and the famous newspaper column under the Goren by-line is now shared by Omar Sharif. The master himself has no need to turn his hand to the plough.

Charles Goren called his bridge tip "Try the Duck."

"If you aren't sure how to continue after you win a trick, you should consider ducking it. But there are many cases when you will not have time for consideration after the opportunity arises—the duck will be effective only if you execute it smoothly, leaving declarer in doubt where the high card is. Examples occur when you, as defender, see only these cards:

(1)   *North*
             K Q 10

                              East
                              A x x

(2)   *North*
             K Q 10

West
A x x

"Declarer plays low toward dummy; and when he plays the Queen, it holds the trick. Who has the Ace?

"Returning to his hand, he leads the suit again, West once more playing low. Which of dummy's cards should declarer play?

"Obviously, unless the Ace is the setting trick and you are in danger of losing it, it must be right for both defenders to duck the first time and for West to play low the second time as well. The alternatives—for East to take the Ace the first time or for West either to take the Ace the second time or to go into a brown study—leave the declarer no problem.

"The next and only slightly more difficult stage of the same situation is this one:

             North
             x x x

West
A x x

"Declarer, South, leads low from dummy and plays the King. If he makes this play early, it will be a mistake to take the Ace—unless you have reason to believe the King is alone. Declarer is unlikely to have chosen to lead up to an unsupported King at such an early stage of the play; he probably has K-Q-10 or K-Q-x. (The lead toward an unsupported King is not an uncommon ruse, especially against strong opposition.—T.R.) Suppose declarer has K-Q-10; if you take the first trick with the Ace, he will later finesse the 10, with no need to guess who holds the Ace.

"Even if declarer holds K-Q-x, it will still pay you to duck whenever dummy is at all short of entries. If you win the first trick, declarer will use dummy's reentry to find some other play that may gain a trick. If you withhold the Ace, he may use that entry in order to repeat his 'successful' first play.

"There are also many less obvious opportunities for ducking plays. Among them is the situation where you can save your partner from a squeeze if you refuse to win a trick. In most squeezes, declarer must be able to win within one trick of the required number. To reach this position, he may endeavor to lose a trick while still retaining control—a process known as 'rectifying the count.' Here is a unique, but by no means difficult-to-fathom, opportunity for East to balk declarer's plan.

South dealer
Neither side vulnerable

North
♠ Q 6 5
♡ 10 9 4
♢ A K 10 9
♣ J 10 9

West
♠ J 10 9 2
♡ Q J 6
♢ 5 3 2
♣ 4 3 2

East
♠ 7 4
♡ 7 5 3 2
♢ 7 6 4
♣ A 8 7 6

South
♠ A K 8 3
♡ A K 8
♢ Q J 8
♣ K Q 5

"South bids 2NT, North raises to 4NT and South goes on to 6NT, against which West opens with the Jack of spades. Declarer wins in his hand with the Ace—which should not fool you. He leads the King of clubs and, sitting East, you duck. Next, he leads the 5 of clubs. It is apparent (from partner's play of the 2 and 3) that South began with only three clubs and very possibly it would suit him to lose this trick, and so rectify the count for a squeeze. So you duck the trick once again! Now he cannot surrender a club trick without letting you cash another. He is forced to abandon clubs and look for his 12th trick in spades or via a squeeze. But when he runs off four diamond tricks, discarding a club from his hand, West is able to discard a club. You will never make your Ace of clubs, but partner will make a trick in hearts and a trick in spades."

Goren went on to explain how West could be squeezed in the major suits if East captured either the first or second round of clubs.

The advice about ducking with A-x-x over (or under) K-Q-10 is fairly basic, and readers of this book may like to look at some more subtle examples of this type of play. Take this very common situation:

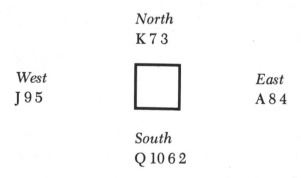

North
K 7 3

West
J 9 5

East
A 8 4

South
Q 10 6 2

Playing in a notrump contract, South leads low to dummy's King. Defenders normally take the trick, but note that as a practical matter, it is not essential to do so. If East ducks, South will finesse the 10 on the way back and still lose two tricks. On many occasions, it will suit the defense better for West to take the first trick. When this is the case, East must not be nervous of allowing the King to hold.

There is another way in which this play may gain. There may be deceptive value in withholding the Ace: declarer may mentally place West with this card and form a wrong picture of the lie of the honors in another suit.

Suppose that East had held A-J-x instead of A-x-x: once again, to win with the Ace does not gain, because South will be finessing the 10 on the next round. Then can it gain *not* to play the Ace from A-J-x? Quite possibly, when the cards lie like this:

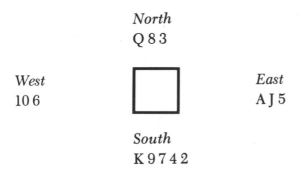

North
Q 8 3

West　　　　　　　　　　　　*East*
10 6　　　　　　　　　　　　A J 5

South
K 9 7 4 2

This is the trump suit and South leads low to the Queen. If there is a possibility that declarer holds a six-card suit, East must win; but if South has only five in the suit, the result will be the same whether East ducks or wins. If the Queen is allowed to hold, South will play back the 3 and will himself duck when East plays the Jack, as he will hope to bring down West's doubleton Ace. It may be to the advantage of the defense for East to gain two entries, and furthermore, after the Jack has held, South will place West with the Ace.

Generally speaking, too, a defender with A-J-10-x in the trump suit should duck the first round. The play is especially successful when declarer plays at low level with a fragile trump suit:

North
Q 8 6

West
A J 10 3

East
9 4

South
K 7 5 2

Declarer would normally prefer to broach this suit by leading low from hand, but the entry situation may cause him to make the first lead from dummy. Now observe the effect if the King is allowed to hold. South returns the 2, West plays the Jack (best) and dummy will duck, allowing West to pull all the trumps.

The idea of a duck to defeat a squeeze is, of course, familiar to practicioners of the art. The ingenious authors of *Right Through the Pack* (published by Allen & Unwin) gave an example that has always stayed in my mind:

North
♠ K Q 7 2
♡ A Q 8 3
◊ K
♣ Q 5 3 2

West
♠ J 9 8 6
♡ K J 10 9
◊ 3
♣ J 9 8 7

East
♠ 5 4 3
♡ 6 5
◊ A Q J 8 7 6 2
♣ 10

South
♠ A 10
♡ 7 4 2
◊ 10 9 5 4
♣ A K 6 4

In face of competition from East, South plays in 4NT and West leads the 3 of diamonds. To defeat the contract, East must allow dummy's King to hold! To take the Ace and switch is not good enough, because declarer will soon lead back the 10 of diamonds, to West's great embarrassment.

THE AWARDS FOR BRIDGE TIPS 1 TO 8

The eight entries for the first competition were assessed by a panel of 27 international experts, all of them members of the International Bridge Press Association and including such stalwarts as C.C. Wei, inventor of the Precision System, B. Jay Becker, and Sammy Kehela. It was not, perhaps, made entirely clear, at the outset, by what criterion the entries should be judged. There were two ways of looking at it:

(a) Was the main object to provide good column material for the journalist members of the IBPA?

or

(b) Was the competition a test to provide useful and comparatively fresh ideas for players of fairly high standard?

To some extent, of course, these objectives overlapped. As a columnist, I could have made more of Robert Hamman's deal than of any other; but if the test was to supply a good bridge tip—something that players tend not to think about—then the choice might fall elsewhere.

Before I reveal the panel's 1-2-3, you may find it an interesting challenge to form your own judgment. At the same time, this will make you think hard about what the tips really mean. To remind you, the entries were:

1. ROBERT HAMMAN: *If you are ever to amount to anything at this game, you must build up a picture of the unseen hands.*

2. RIXI MARKUS: *When, as a defender, you are about to attack from a holding such as J-x, Q-x, or K-x, consider the possible advantage of leading a low card.*

3. GABRIEL CHAGAS: *When you have to develop a shaky suit, consider whether you can prepare for an intra-finesse by ducking with an 8 or a 9 on the first round.*

4. TERENCE REESE: *Study the early discards and consider this point: from what holding would the defender most readily have made those discards?*

5. TIM SERES: *When you can see that declarer is bound to succeed by normal play, look for a chance to give him a losing option.*

6. GIORGIO BELLADONNA: *When, as a defender, you hold the Ace of trumps, consider whether to hold up this card when trumps are first played.*

7. BOBBY WOLFF: *Do not be content simply to work out the high cards a defender is likely to hold: try to assess his distribution as well.*

8. CHARLES GOREN: *As a defender, consider the advantage of ducking to conceal the lie of the cards or to spoil the timing for a squeeze.*

Do not, as they say, read on, until you have reached your own verdict.

The 27 judges were empowered to award up to 20 points for each entry, so the possible total was 540. The scores for the first three, who won the major prizes, were:

1. *Terence Reese* (study the discards), 425 points.

2. *Gabriel Chagas* (intra-finesses), 384 points.

3. *Tim Seres* (give declarer enough rope), 377 points.

If the main object was to provide a useful tip rather than scintillating column material, then, casting modesty aside, I think that my entry, because of its wide application, did have an edge. Rixi's hint was original and specific, and might well have won a prize.

The entries from the three American players all contained good hands and dealt with important themes, but they were perhaps of too general a nature to catch the eye of the judges. Belladonna's theme was a good one, too, but his examples were of a familiar kind.

Chagas, the runner-up, dealt interestingly with a form of play that has seldom been identified, and Tim Seres, third, described some good deceptive plays that would be new, if not to the journalists, to a high proportion of readers.

9. HOWARD SCHENKEN (U.S.A.)

"When on defense in third position, cultivate the habit of playing slowly to the first trick."

Howard Schenken, sad to relate, died early in 1979, after a career as long as contract bridge itself. He and Mike Gottlieb each played a session with Ely Culbertson in the "Bridge Battle of the Century," the Culbertson-Lenz match of 1931. Soon after, these two became a famous partnership in the Four Aces team. As a pair, they visited England in 1935 and demolished the opposition.

Gottlieb gave up bridge for business, but Schenken stayed at the top for about 45 years. His record in major ACBL championships is unapproached: 10 wins in the Spingold, 10 in the Vanderbilt, 5 in the Life Masters Pairs for the Von Zedtwitz Gold Cup. He also won the first three Bermuda Bowl championships and competed in several more. He wrote two books on his one club system, and related his experiences in *The Education of a Bridge Player.*

Howard was tall, spare, and very relaxed in speech and manner. He kindly asked me to write a foreword to the English edition of the *Big Club*, which characteristically was dedicated "To Bee, my wife and favorite partner." My piece ended:

"It is a special pleasure to me to introduce a book by Howard Schenken. I first saw him play, as a callow undergraduate, in a challenge match at the Dorchester when he was a star of the Four Aces. He played then with a relaxed and easy command that has remained the same over the years. In America, he is known as the 'experts' expert.' The story goes that a magazine asked 20 leading players to compile a ranking list, all modesty apart. There was one consistent feature in the ratings: 2—Howard Schenken."

Howard called his bridge tip "On Defense at Trick One:"

"Much has been written about the careful thought required of declarer before he plays to the first trick. But little has been said about the player at the declarer's right—East in the normal diagram.

"When you are in this position, you often have a difficult but vital role to play. Unlike declarer, you cannot see your partner's hand, but by reviewing the bidding and observing the lead, you may be able to visualize it.

"While South is thinking over his plan of attack, you may have a chance to plan your defense. Even if South plays quickly to the first trick, you should not allow yourself to be hurried. For example:

North
♠ 9 5
♡ J 10 4
◇ K Q 2
♣ A 10 7 5 3

West

♡ led

East
♠ J 10 7 2
♡ Q 8 5 3
◇ A 9 4
♣ K 6

"South opens a strong notrump, North raised to 3NT, and West led the 2 of hearts. Declarer quickly plays dummy's 10, and of course, you cover with the Queen automatically. Or do you? Not unless you have been lulled into following suit without thinking.

"So I will assume you are concentrating and are ready to begin the chore of counting points. You and dummy each have 10, South has at least 16, so your partner has at most 4. His fourth-best lead shows a four-card suit with (a) no honors, (b) the King, (c) the Ace.

"If (a) you lose a trick by covering; with (b) you break even. So you focus your attention on (c), which gives declarer K-x. In this case, of course, you must duck, and when sooner or later you come in with the King of clubs, your heart return defeats the contract.

"Even when you have an automatic play to the first trick, you can still pause and say, 'Sorry, I'm not think-ing about this trick.' This may help you prepare for a vital decision at the next trick, as in this example:

North
♠ 7 6 5
♡ 9 2
♢ K J 10 9 8 7
♣ A 3

West
♠ Q led

East
♠ A 3
♡ J 10 8 7
♢ A 6 5
♣ K J 10 9

"South opens with 1NT, North raises to 3NT and partner opens with the Queen of spades. Counting points presents no problem. You have 13, the dummy 8, and partner's lead has shown 3. The total is 24, and since declarer surely has 15—more likely 16—you are on your own as sole defender.

"Now you turn your attention to tricks. If declarer can bring in the diamond suit, he will romp home. But as you gaze at the dummy, you notice that the Ace is only once guarded. The light dawns! Triumphantly, you win the first trick with the Ace of spades and lead the King of clubs. As Muhammad Ali would say, 'The Ace will fall in two rounds.'

"Note that the King of clubs cannot possibly give declarer a ninth trick: at most, he will make one spade, three hearts, two diamonds, and two clubs.

"The next hand is difficult and requires careful planning. Please cover the West and South hands.

South dealer
Both sides vulnerable

                    North
                    ♠ A 9 6 2
                    ♡ A 3 2
                    ◊ Q 5
                    ♣ Q 10 8 6

West   *East*
♠ 10 8 7 3   ┌─────────┐   ♠ K J 5
♡ 5   │   │   ♡ K 8 7 6 4
◊ A 9 6 2   │   │   ◊ K 10 8 3
♣ 7 5 4 2   └─────────┘   ♣ 9

                    South
                    ♠ Q 4
                    ♡ Q J 10 9
                    ◊ J 7 4
                    ♣ A K J 3

                    South   *North*
                     1♡   1♠
                     1NT   3NT
                     Pass

"West leads the 2 of diamonds and declarer plays dummy's 5. Plan the defense in detail.

"From the bidding and lead, you deduce that partner's distribution is probably 4-1-4-4. If his lead is from the Jack, your 10 will force the Ace. But if partner had the Jack, declarer would have played dummy's Queen, hoping to hold the trick!

"So you conclude that your King will win and that you can establish three diamond tricks. You can certainly expect to make the King of hearts, but you will still need at least one trick in spades. With this in mind, you win the King of diamonds and return the 8, thereby deceiving partner into thinking that South started with J-10-7-4!

"This produces the desired result as partner wins with the Ace of diamonds and shifts to a spade. Declarer perforce plays low from dummy and you win with the King. Now you shift back to diamonds and are ready to take the setting trick when you get in with the King of hearts. You apologize to partner for your deceit, but he forgives you readily, since no other defense would have set this contract.

"My tip therefore is this: when on defense in third position, cultivate the habit of playing slowly to the first trick. Careful thought will help you defeat many more contracts."

This last deal was exceptionally difficult. Who would think of returning the 8 of diamonds, so that partner would place the declarer with J-10-x-x? When Howard's article first appeared in the *IBPA Bulletin*, I dutifully covered the West and South hands and found an alternative answer of sorts—the Jack of spades at trick two. If declarer held Q-x-x and placed East with J-10-8, he might allow the Jack to hold. The analysis doesn't quite stand up in the present case, I know, because declarer cannot afford to concede a spade trick at this point. However, the type of play—Jack from K-J-x—is worth noting. This is another play of the same kind:

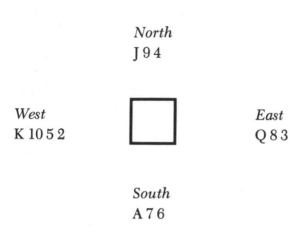

North
J 9 4

West
K 10 5 2

East
Q 8 3

South
A 7 6

East, on lead, needs to establish two tricks in this suit. The bold play of the Queen (similarly the King from K-x-x) will almost always succeed. Placing the leader with K-Q-10, the declarer will play a Bath coup—and get wet!

Returning to the general subject of Howard's Bols Tip, note in particular his advice that the third player should make a habit of counting the points when dummy goes down, so that he will have a picture of how much may be expected from partner. This practice will put the defender on the track of many a killing defense.

North
♠ K J 8 7
♡ K 5 2
♢ Q 9 8 5 3
♣ 8

West

♡ Q led

East
♠ Q 10 3
♡ 8 4 2
♢ K J
♣ A 9 7 6 3

South opens a strong notrump and lands in four spades after a Stayman inquiry. When dummy goes down, East adds his own 10 points to declarer's expected minimum of 16. At best, his partner may hold the Queen of clubs in addition to ♡ Q-J. To beat the contract, it will be necessary to come to a heart trick, in addition to a diamond, a club, and a trump. Accordingly, when South wins in dummy and leads the singleton club, East must duck, hoping that South holding ♣ K-J, will finesse the Jack. If East were to put up the Ace of clubs, the contract would surely be made, as a heart from dummy would go away on the King of clubs.

The Norwegian writer, Helge Vinje, in *New Ideas in Defensive Play*, published by Robert Hale, makes some very good points about the play by third hand.

Consider this common position:

North
753

West   [ ]   *East*
A 10 8 4 2   J 9 6

South
K Q

What usually happens is that West, defending against notrumps, leads low to the Jack and King (or Queen), and when West obtains the lead, he is nervous of laying down the Ace. Vinje's system is that East, when he can place declarer with a doubleton, should play low, not the Jack. Then West need have no qualms about leading the Ace when he comes in, and East will, of course, unblock.

This is another situation of the same sort, where the best play is seldom recognized:

North
8

West   [ ]   *East*
A 9 7 5 3   Q J 10 2

South
K 6 4

West leads low and the 10 loses to the King. When West gains the lead, he may be afraid to continue, since East may hold J-10-x, and declarer K-Q-x. There is advantage for East in playing the *Jack* on the first round. Then, from West's angle, it can do no harm to lead low when next in: either partner has Q-J-x or declarer has K-Q-10.

A subtle reason for unusual play by third hand occurs on this deal:

West dealer
Both sides vulnerable

North
♠ K 9 3
♡ Q 6 2
◇ 8 5 4
♣ K J 8 6

West
♠ J 8
♡ K 8 4
◇ K J 9 7 3
♣ A 10 2

East
♠ Q 7 5 4
♡ J 10 5
◇ 10 6 2
♣ 7 5 3

South
♠ A 10 6 2
♡ A 9 7 3
◇ A Q
♣ Q 9 4

South	West	North	East
—	1 ◇	Pass	Pass
Dble	Pass	2 ♣	Pass
2NT	Pass	3NT	Pass
Pass	Pass		

West's lead of the 7 of diamonds goes to the 10 and Queen. South forces out the Ace of clubs, and West returns the King of diamonds, clearing the suit. Declarer cashes his winners in the black suits, West discarding a heart on the fourth club, then exits with dummy's 8 of diamonds. West makes three diamond tricks, but has to lead from the King of hearts at the finish.

What could the defense have done about this? Well, East must not play the 10 of diamonds on the first trick. Now West cannot be end-played, because East wins the third diamond and exits with a heart.

10. JEREMY FLINT (ENGLAND)

"Instead of stolidly pushing out an unimaginative small card from three or four to an honor, you should consider whether to lead the honor."

Like many of the top bridge players, Jeremy Flint set forth on a legal career, but decided that progress would be slow and that his future lay in bridge. He soon made an impression in the tournament world, playing mostly in the early days with Tony Priday. In 1960, he was in the British team that finished second in the Olympiad at Turin, and ever since then, he has been an automatic choice, winning the European at Baden-Baden in 1963, finishing third in the 1964 Olympiad and third again (under my dynamic leadership!) at Monte Carlo in 1976. He has been equally successful in pairs events. In 1965, he played on the American tournament circuit with Peter Pender and created a record by becoming a Life Master of the ACBL in 11 weeks. A few years later, he and I won the Masters Pairs three times in four years.

Jeremy is a notable theorist. Apart from the Flint convention, which is widely played throughout the world, he developed the Flint-Pender system, described in his ferocious *Tiger Bridge.* He currently plays an advanced version of Precision.

In another book I said: "With long, fair hair and a

high, thin nose, he could put on a top hat and look like an Edwardian man-about-town. In certain ways, I see a reflection of myself. Jeremy has the same dislike of regular toil. He is prepared for any kind of speculative venture on which he can bring his intelligence to bear."

His tip is entitled "Consider Whether to Lead an Honor":

"It is normal in bridge to lead low from a suit of three or more cards headed by an unsupported honor card. There are, however, some basic situations where the lead of a high card may produce better results.

"The most common of these occurs when there has been a competitive auction. Suppose that the defender on the lead has, say, K-x-x-x of his partner's suit and scarcely any other assets. It may very well be good play to start with the *King* in order to retain the lead and find the killing switch through the dummy.

Here is a case where more thought is required:

South	North
1♣	1♠
2♦	2♠
2NT	3NT
Pass	

"West has to lead from:

♠ K 10 7
♡ Q 10 4
♢ Q 3 2
♣ J 9 7 6

"The opponents' bidding suggests that they have very little to spare. Furthermore, South has displayed lukewarm enthusiasm for his partner's suit. For that reason, it is good play to attack with a spade. No other lead appeals and declarer may well be embarrassed by an early assault on dummy's entry.

"Having reached that conclusion, the best card to lead is the *King*. Declarer may misjudge the lie of the suit—or the King may even score a trick by force. In play, this was the full deal:

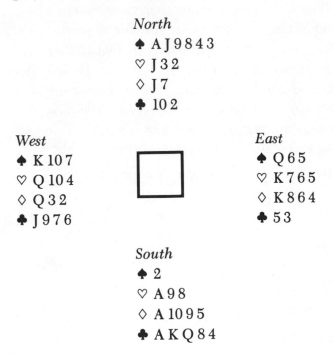

North
♠ A J 9 8 4 3
♡ J 3 2
◇ J 7
♣ 10 2

West
♠ K 10 7
♡ Q 10 4
◇ Q 3 2
♣ J 9 7 6

East
♠ Q 6 5
♡ K 7 6 5
◇ K 8 6 4
♣ 5 3

South
♠ 2
♡ A 9 8
◇ A 10 9 5
♣ A K Q 8 4

"Not unnaturally, declarer allowed the King of spades to win. On the next trick, he received a nasty shock when the Jack lost to the Queen. He elected to discard a heart. Now, after a heart switch and continuation, he was held to six tricks. At the other table, after a heart opening lead, South succeeded in scrambling home with two heart tricks, four clubs, two diamonds, and a spade.

All the assets

"Sometimes a defender will possess practically all of his side's assets and yet have no attractive opening lead at his disposal. Here is a typical example:

South dealer
Neither side vulnerable

```
                      North
                      ♠ K 7 4
                      ♡ A 10 4
                      ◊ A 8 7 4 3
                      ♣ 7 2

West                                    East
♠ Q 10 2                                ♠ 8 6 5
♡ Q 9 5               ┌─────┐           ♡ J 7 3 2
◊ K J 9 6            │     │            ◊ 10 5
♣ A Q 3             └─────┘           ♣ 8 6 5 4

                      South
                      ♠ A J 9 3
                      ♡ K 8 6
                      ◊ Q 2
                      ♣ K J 10 9
```

"The bidding has been:

South	North
1♣	1♢
1♠	2♡
2NT	3NT
Pass	

"North's two hearts is artificial, in the fourth-suit-forcing style. With no attractive alternatives, West decides to lead this suit.

"It is easy for West to appreciate that East can have—at most—one or two points. Unless East has an honor in hearts, it will be immaterial which heart West chooses to lead. However, if East happens to have the Jack, the *Queen* will be the superior lead for three reasons. First, declarer may well misjudge the lie of the suit. Secondly, the presence of the 9 in West's hand means that declarer's options in the suit will be restricted. Finally, if declarer does go wrong, the effect will be to create a vital entry in East's hand. This last consideration is of prime importance, since in this type of hand, West is all too likely to find himself repeatedly on play.

"In our example, declarer wins the lead of the Queen of hearts in his own hand, goes to dummy with the King of spades and leads a club, losing the 9 to West's Queen. West continues with a heart, which East wins. Appreciating that his own hand is dead, East switches to a diamond, and now the contract is doomed.

"It is clear that if West starts with a low heart instead of the Queen, East will never gain the lead, and declarer is likely to come home a winner without ever being seriously threatened.

"My tip, therefore, is that instead of stolidly pushing out an unimaginative small card from three or four to an honor, you should consider whether to lead the honor."

Yes, indeed, I have always thought that the lead of a low card from three to an honor, against a suit contract, was overdone. This applies especially when the leader holds K-x-x. Suppose that a suit the defense has bid and supported lies like this:

	North	
	x x	
West		*East*
K x x		A J 10 x x x
	South	
	Q x	

If, as West, you lead low, partner won't know whether to play a second round or not. If he fails to do so, the loser may disappear; if he does return the suit, and finds that declarer has K-x instead of Q-x, he may be losing a vital tempo. For clarity, therefore, I like to lead the King from K-x-x in these positions.

The lead of an honor is to be recommended also, whenever the dummy hand is more likely (perhaps having bid notrumps) to have a guarded honor than the declarer. The distribution of the side suit may be:

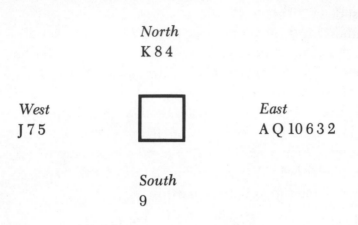

North
K 8 4

West
J 7 5

East
A Q 10 6 3 2

South
9

Here the lead of a low card, instead of the Jack, can ruin the defense: they lose the chance for a forcing game, and East cannot exit in the suit when he gains the lead.

Flint described three occasions where the lead of a high card is indicated:

(1) When the defender has something like K-x-x-x and a weak hand, so that he may never again hold the lead;

(2) When declarer is marked with a shortage—often it is possible to pin an honor card, a singleton Jack or Queen;

(3) When the opening leader is strong all-round and must guard against being end-played.

There was a classic example of the second of these situations in the 1976 Bermuda Bowl:

West dealer
Neither side vulnerable

North
♠ 10 5 3 2
♡ A 7
◇ 3
♣ A J 10 7 5 2

West
♠ A Q 6
♡ K 10 6 3
◇ 9 8 5 4
♣ 8 6

East
♠ J 9 8 7 4
♡ 8 4 2
◇ K 6 2
♣ Q 9

South
♠ K
♡ Q J 9 5
◇ A Q J 10 7
♣ K 4 3

The Italians in the closed room played in 3NT from the North side, and a spade lead from East gave the defense five tricks. A gain for America seemed likely when, on Vu-Graph, the hand was played the other way up:

South	West	North	East
Rubin	Franco	Soloway	Garozzo
—	Pass	Pass	Pass
1♦	Pass	2♣	Pass
2♦	Pass	2♠	Pass
3NT	Pass	Pass	Pass

There was no swing, however, because Franco, judging that the best chance lay in spades and that South would be short, made the brilliant lead of the Ace of spades. "What a pleasure to have screens," remarked Edgar Kaplan in the *Bridge World*, meaning that on this occasion no one could cast aspersions.

11. JAMES JACOBY (U.S.A.)

"When a good opponent seemingly gives you a present—stay alert! Watch for a trap! Beware bridge players bringing gifts!"

James Jacoby is the son of the famous Oswald Jacoby, who played a leading role in the "Bridge Battle of the Century," which I mentioned earlier. Ossie, of course, is a master of many games and has written fine books on poker and backgammon, as well as bridge; so son Jim had everything in favor when he began his career.

Jim, a Texan, was one of the original Dallas Aces. He was world champion in 1970 and 1971, and has a long string of successes in the Spingold and Vanderbilt. He is now one of the most professional of North American player-writers, sharing a widely syndicated bridge column with his father.

Jim smokes large cigars at a rakish angle, and you could picture him riding the range in a ten-gallon hat. Here is how he developed his engaging Bols Tip:

"You bridge players do a lot of humdrum and routine work. Consequently, it's very easy for you to be lulled into that well-known false sense of security. Of course, in theory, you should play your heart out on every deal—but as a practical matter you just don't.

"It helps to get the adrenalin going—but how do you do it? This is a problem you must solve individually. But perhaps I can help some of the time with a tale from an old legend.

"In Virgil's *Aeneid*, the soothsayer, Cassandra, warned the Trojan warriors: 'Timeo Danaos et dona ferentes.' (I fear the Greeks, even bearing gifts.) Nevertheless, when they saw that the retreating Greeks had left behind them a large wooden horse, they couldn't resist taking it into their city—and we know what that led to! Virgil, or Homer before him, little knew that the story of the Trojan horse could assist bridge players thousands of years later. So, with due acknowledgment to the ancient poets, my Bols Tip is: 'Beware bridge players bringing gifts.'

"There is a wealth of deals with Trojan horse themes. Here is one from a recent team-of-four final at a U.S. regional tournament:

"The opening lead was the 3 of spades. Declarer won with dummy's King and played off the K-Q of clubs. When East showed out on the second club lead, there were only eight tricks in sight. But declarer sent his wooden horse to the gates of Troy. He led the Jack of diamonds from dummy. East disappointed his admirers watching on Vu-Graph by cashing four rounds of diamonds. He might as well have leant across the table and strangled his partner. West threw two spades on the diamonds, but had no good discard when the Ace of spades was played."

East dealer
Both sides vulnerable

North
- ♠ K 2
- ♡ K Q 7 3
- ◇ J 10 2
- ♣ K Q 4 2

West
- ♠ Q 9 3
- ♡ J 10 6 2
- ◇ 6 5
- ♣ J 9 8 5

East
- ♠ J 10 7 5 4
- ♡ 9 5 4
- ◇ A K Q 9
- ♣ 6

South
- ♠ A 8 6
- ♡ A 8
- ◇ 8 7 4 3
- ♣ A 10 7 3

South	West	North	East
—	—	—	Pass
1♣	Pass	1♡	Dble
Pass	1♠	2♠	Pass
2NT	Pass	3NT	Pass
Pass	Pass		

As astute readers will have noted, West is always going to be a loser on this deal, because of his minor tenace in clubs; however, the defensive point is sound and has wide application. Jacoby continued:

"Next we have a familiar theme:

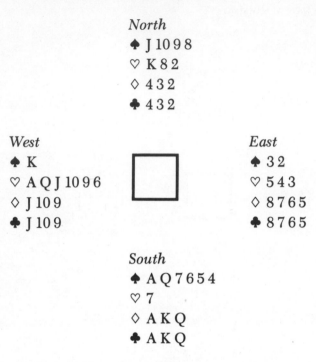

North
♠ J 10 9 8
♡ K 8 2
◇ 4 3 2
♣ 4 3 2

West
♠ K
♡ A Q J 10 9 6
◇ J 10 9
♣ J 10 9

East
♠ 3 2
♡ 5 4 3
◇ 8 7 6 5
♣ 8 7 6 5

South
♠ A Q 7 6 5 4
♡ 7
◇ A K Q
♣ A K Q

"South plays in six spades after West has overcalled in hearts. West leads the Ace of hearts and continues with a second heart, putting the lead in the North hand so that declarer can (hopefully) take a losing trump finesse. But now that you are aware of the clever traps these bridge players set, you simply play the spade Ace—and sneer as the King comes clattering down.

"An exciting demonstration of the wooden horse ploy occurred in the 1971 world team championship, held in Taiwan. Bobby Wolff was the star. The hapless victims were Svarc and Boulenger, of France.

South dealer
Neither side vulnerable

North
♠ K 8 5
♡ K 10 3
◊ A Q J 3 2
♣ J 7

West
♠ A 10 6
♡ Q 9 6 2
◊ 8 6
♣ K 9 5 2

East
♠ J 9 4 2
♡ 5
◊ 9 7 5 4
♣ A 10 8 4

South
♠ Q 7 3
♡ A J 8 7 4
◊ K 10
♣ Q 6 3

"Wolff became declarer in four hearts after this bidding:

South	West	North	East
Wolff	Svarc	Jacoby	Boulenger
1♡	Pass	2◊	Pass
2♡	Pass	4♡	Pass
Pass	Pass		

"West led the 2 of clubs to his partner's Ace. After brief reflection, Boulenger returned a low club. Svarc won with the King, cashed Ace of spades, and led another spade.

"From South's angle, there was no certainty that a bridge gift had been offered—and yet, would Svarc have cashed the Ace of spades unless he felt there was some good chance of taking the setting trick later? (Without such expectation, he might, for example, have played a low spade, hoping to find East with the Queen; the Ace of spades would also be a mistake if South held something like ♠ Q-x, ♡ A-Q-J-x-x-x ◊ 10-x ♣ Q-x-x.)

"So there were good reasons already to place West with the guarded Queen of hearts. At any rate, Wolff won the spade in hand with the Queen and led ♡ J, which was covered by West and won in dummy. Declarer came back to hand with ◊ 10 and led ♡ 8. When Svarc played low, Wolff called for the 3! How did it all happen?

"Simple enough. Declarer decided, first, that the prompt play of the Ace of spades marked West with the Queen of hearts. Then, when West covered the Jack, there was a further deduction that he did not hold Q-x or Q-x-x, since a player with that trump holding would not reveal the Queen. So the play of ♡ Q was a gift: a gift that tested the declarer. Fortunately, for the Aces' world championship aspirations that year, Wolff passed the test.

"Remember this Bols Tip to win: when a good opponent seemingly gives you a present—stay alert! Watch for a trap! Beware bridge players bearing gifts."

Note how Bobby Wolff's play of this deal accorded with his own tip, "Do not be content simply to work out the high cards a defender is likely to hold: try to assess his distribution as well."

Jacoby describes, in his first deal, how a defender is tricked into squeezing his partner. Here the declarer plays on the opponent's best suit for a different reason:

North
♠ 7 5 3
♡ 8 6
◊ K 7 5 3 2
♣ J 10 4

West
♠ Q 10 8
♡ J 9 5 2
◊ 6
♣ A Q 8 5 2

East
♠ J 9 6 4
♡ K Q 3
◊ J 10 4
♣ 9 7 6

South
♠ A K 2
♡ A 10 7 4
◊ A Q 9 8
♣ K 3

South opens 2NT and North raises to 3NT. West leads the 5 of clubs, described as fourth-best, and dummy's Jack holds the first trick. South immediately returns a club!

West must not cash even one more club, for this will give South a chance to dispose of the obstructing 8 of diamonds. West must switch to a heart (or, as the cards lie, a spade) and declarer, with the diamonds blocked, will be unable to develop a ninth trick.

Note that it is good play for South to return the club immediately. If he first tests the diamonds, then the intention of his "Trojan horse" play is more evident to the defense.

In his second deal, Jacoby illustrated the free offer to take a finesse—an offer which declarer should refuse. Somewhat similar is the situation in a trump contract when a side suit is divided in this way:

North
K J 7 4

West
109863

East
Q 5 2

South
A

West leads the 10 to declarer's Ace, and as soon as he gains the lead, West advances the 9 of the same suit. You will often see a declarer finesse, on the grounds that this is mathematically the best chance to win an extra trick; but it is much more likely that the defender is seeking to deflect the declarer from playing King and another, bringing down the Queen.

12. JEAN BESSE (SWITZERLAND)

"Beware of your trump tricks. When you see a chance for an easy overruff, don't be in too much of a hurry to take it."

Jean Besse, of Switzerland, is one of the fixed lights of European bridge. He has played in more European Championships than any other player. A Swiss team without him would be like Hamlet without the Prince. Switzerland has often been in a challenging position in the European Championship, but has never quite won the title. The country's best Olympiad performance was fifth place in New York in 1964.

In 1954, Besse, and the legendary Karl Schneider, were enlisted by the French, winners of the European that year, to represent Europe against the U.S.A. in the Bermuda Bowl. The experiment was a mixed success and since then, Europe has always been represented by a complete team from the winning country.

I first met Jean in Paris, during the 1949 championship—before Switzerland had begun to compete. I remember Boris Schapiro saying to me, "This Jean has our sense of humor." This indeed turned out to be the case—his owlish look, the rising inflexions of his voice, and nervous coughs, or ahems, adding to the comic effect of his discourse.

A mathematician with brilliant qualities of mind, Jean has made his career in the computer world. He is a bridge player of unsurpassed inventiveness, as is evident from his column in the *Journal de Geneve* and from his Bols Tip, entitled "Beware of Your Trump Tricks." By "beware of" he means, be sure you put them to the best possible use.

"Bobby Fischer once said: 'You have found a very good move. Fine! This is the time to think again: *there probably exists a better one.*'

"Bobby, of course, was talking about chess. His advice, however, applies also to bridge—and especially to the situation where a defender sees an opportunity to make an easy trump trick. Surprisingly often, it will pay him to look for better things.

"Players soon learn that by not overruffing the Queen with K-10-2 behind declarer's A-Q-J-9-8-7, they can ensure two tricks. The following, however, is less obvious:

"The contract is four spades. South ruffs the opening club lead and sets out to establish his side suit: he takes two top hearts and ruffs a heart in dummy with the Queen of spades.

"If East yields to the temptation of overruffing with the King, South loses only one other trump trick and makes his contract.

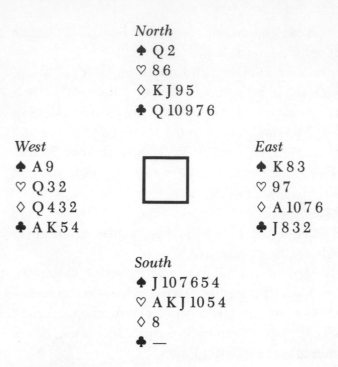

North
- ♠ Q 2
- ♡ 8 6
- ◇ K J 9 5
- ♣ Q 10 9 7 6

West
- ♠ A 9
- ♡ Q 3 2
- ◇ Q 4 3 2
- ♣ A K 5 4

East
- ♠ K 8 3
- ♡ 9 7
- ◇ A 10 7 6
- ♣ J 8 3 2

South
- ♠ J 10 7 6 5 4
- ♡ A K J 10 5 4
- ◇ 8
- ♣ —

"But if East refuses to overruff, the declarer is bound to lose three trump tricks no matter how hard he tries. With a diamond loser in addition, he is defeated.

"The idea of not overruffing soon becomes familiar whenever you hold either length or strength in the trump suit. Somewhat less well known are those cases where the defender *with the shorter or weaker trump holding* may gain a trick for his side by employing the same tactics.

"South plays in four spades after East has overcalled in hearts. West leads the 10 of hearts and East plays off the three top cards in the suit.

```
                    North
                    ♠ 9 2
                    ♡ 6 5
                    ◊ A K Q 4 3
                    ♣ A K 5 4

West                                    East
♠ Q 7                                   ♠ K 6 5
♡ 10 7          ┌─────┐                 ♡ A K Q 9 8 2
◊ 10 9 8 7 2    │     │                 ◊ J 5
♣ J 9 6 2       └─────┘                 ♣ 10 8

                    South
                    ♠ A J 10 8 4 3
                    ♡ J 4 3
                    ◊ 6
                    ♣ Q 7 3
```

"If, on the third round of hearts, West jumps in with ♣Q, declarer will discard from dummy and thereafter will have no trouble picking up East's trumps. Instead, West should rise to the occasion by discarding a diamond! After ruffing this trick in dummy, South will have to lose two trump tricks—and his contract.

"In that example, refusal to ruff with the Queen in front of dummy's 9-2 was no more than good technique. Dare you go one step further? It is possible to blend the technique of trump promotion with *deception*, as in this example:

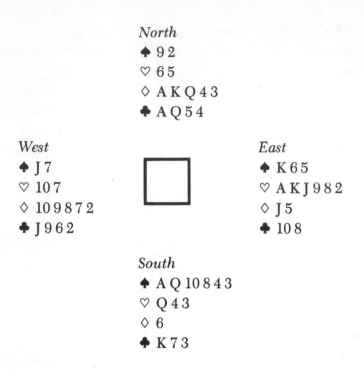

North
- ♠ 9 2
- ♡ 6 5
- ◇ A K Q 4 3
- ♣ A Q 5 4

West
- ♠ J 7
- ♡ 10 7
- ◇ 10 9 8 7 2
- ♣ J 9 6 2

East
- ♠ K 6 5
- ♡ A K J 9 8 2
- ◇ J 5
- ♣ 10 8

South
- ♠ A Q 10 8 4 3
- ♡ Q 4 3
- ◇ 6
- ♣ K 7 3

"Again the contract is four spades, and West leads the 10 of hearts, East playing off Ace, King, and a small one. On the third round, West ruffs declarer's Queen *with the 7 of spades!*

"Declarer overruffs with dummy's 9 and continues with the 2. When East follows with a small trump, declarer is confronted with a problem. If he goes up with the Ace, he may lose two trump tricks to East's possible K-J-x. If he plays the Queen, he may lose to West's possible K-x (for with this holding, West would certainly ruff low, not with the King).

"Declarer may very well decide that his best chance is to finesse with the 10, which seems to take care of both possibilities. It will be a shock to him when the 10 loses to the now singleton Jack, and he has to lose to the King as well.

"Even when you hold only a single isolated trump, and this is of lowly rank, you should still think twice before overruffing with it. Being now in full command of the subject, you will easily manage East's hand in my final example:

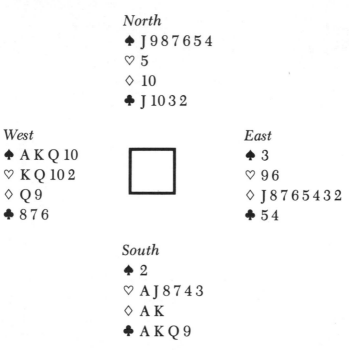

North
♠ J 9 8 7 6 5 4
♡ 5
♢ 10
♣ J 10 3 2

West
♠ A K Q 10
♡ K Q 10 2
♢ Q 9
♣ 8 7 6

East
♠ 3
♡ 9 6
♢ J 8 7 6 5 4 3 2
♣ 5 4

South
♠ 2
♡ A J 8 7 4 3
♢ A K
♣ A K Q 9

"The contract is five clubs, and West begins with two top spades, South ruffing. Declarer cashes the Ace of hearts and ruffs a heart with the 10, since East has discarded a heart on the second spade and threatens to overruff. Declarer continues with a club to the King and a heart ruff with the Jack. After a diamond to the Ace, the position is:

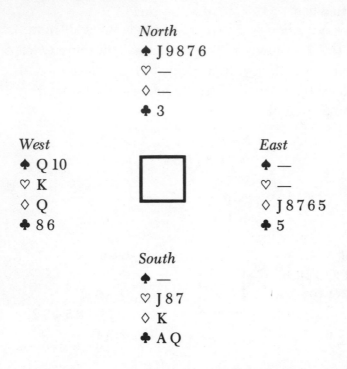

North
♠ J 9 8 7 6
♡ —
♦ —
♣ 3

West
♠ Q 10
♡ K
♦ Q
♣ 8 6

East
♠ —
♡ —
♦ J 8 7 6 5
♣ 5

South
♠ —
♡ J 8 7
♦ K
♣ A Q

"South leads a fourth round of hearts and ruffs with the three. If you now, as East, overruff with your five-spot, you will have to lead diamonds to South's King, enabling him to draw trumps and claim the contract.

"But you, of course, refuse the naive overruff! This leaves declarer locked in dummy, compelled to force his own hand in spades and lose the last two tricks to the 8 of trumps and the Queen of spades.

"My bridge tip is this: beware of your trump tricks. When you see a chance for an easy overruff, don't be in too much of a hurry to take it. You may gain still more tricks by holding back."

In a later issue of the *IBPA Bulletin*, Besse followed this rich offering with another example:

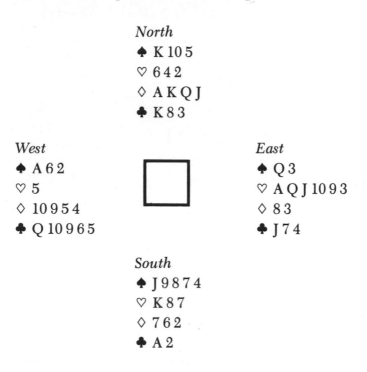

North
♠ K 10 5
♡ 6 4 2
♢ A K Q J
♣ K 8 3

West
♠ A 6 2
♡ 5
♢ 10 9 5 4
♣ Q 10 9 6 5

East
♠ Q 3
♡ A Q J 10 9 3
♢ 8 3
♣ J 7 4

South
♠ J 9 8 7 4
♡ K 8 7
♢ 7 6 2
♣ A 2

North opens 1NT in fourth hand, East overcalls with two hearts, and South become declarer in four spades.

West leads his singleton heart, East plays the Ace and returns the Queen, which is covered by the King. West ruffs and then . . . but there is no hereafter! As East passed originally, South gauges the trumps correctly, and East never comes in to cash his heart.

From West's angle, the best hope is to find partner with a trump entry. If he declines to ruff, or ruffs with the Ace, he enables partner to gain entry with the Queen of spades.

Jean might like to add this deal to his collection:

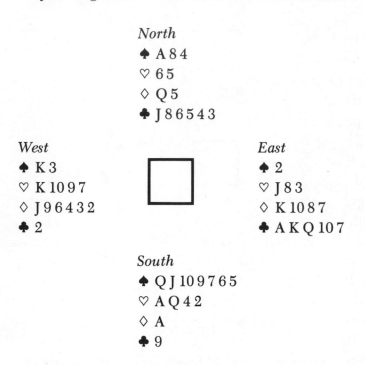

North
♠ A 8 4
♡ 6 5
◇ Q 5
♣ J 8 6 5 4 3

West
♠ K 3
♡ K 10 9 7
◇ J 9 6 4 3 2
♣ 2

East
♠ 2
♡ J 8 3
◇ K 10 8 7
♣ A K Q 10 7

South
♠ Q J 10 9 7 6 5
♡ A Q 4 2
◇ A
♣ 9

Playing in four spades, South ruffs the second club with the Queen. West discards a diamond! South should play Ace and another heart now, but if instead, he crosses to the Ace of trumps and finesses the Queen of hearts, he loses the contract. West wins and cashes his trump winner, leaving declarer with two heart losers and only one trump in dummy.

13. PIETRO FORQUET (ITALY)

"Count the opponents' hands—but when you have counted them, play intelligently."

Pietro Forquet scored his first European Championship victory at Venice in 1951, looking for all the world like a brown-haired, fresh-faced English schoolboy. Thirty years later, winner of innumerable world championships and an important figure in the banking world, he still has a youthful, almost innocent, air.

His main partners have been Chiaradia, Siniscalco, and Garozzo, and with each, he has forced a partnership of outstanding quality. He has had successes also with the other famous Italians, Avarelli and Belladonna.

Forquet is not a thruster, like Garozzo or Belladonna. He is like a tennis player or golfer who just goes on and on, never seeming to make a mistake. Such players are very hard to beat at any game.

Italians are supposed to be temperamental, but Pietro never shows the slightest emotion. He is what the sporting journalists call "a model for any young player." There was the famous occasion at Stockholm, in 1956, when he and Siniscalco had a misunderstanding at the level of seven and played in 7NT doubled with no guard in the opponents' long suit, which was duly cashed. Not a word was said and they proceeded to the next deal as though nothing unusual had happened. Their French opponents were more shaken than they were!

Forquet's tip is entitled "Count the Opponents' Hands, But . . ."

"How many times have you heard the excuse, 'Sorry, partner, if I'd guessed correctly I'd have made the contract'? And how many times was this so-called unlucky guess truly unlucky?

"For example, take a look at a hand that my partner played in a recent pairs event:

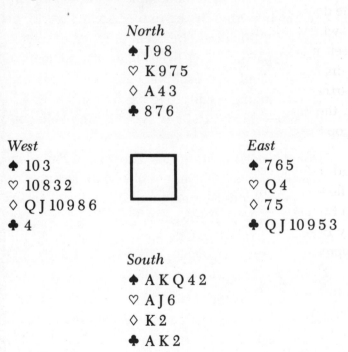

North
♠ J 9 8
♡ K 9 7 5
♢ A 4 3
♣ 8 7 6

West
♠ 10 3
♡ 10 8 3 2
♢ Q J 10 9 8 6
♣ 4

East
♠ 7 6 5
♡ Q 4
♢ 7 5
♣ Q J 10 9 5 3

South
♠ A K Q 4 2
♡ A J 6
♢ K 2
♣ A K 2

"We reached the good contract of six spades, my partner playing the hand as South. West led his singleton club and East's 9 was headed by the Ace. Declarer drew three rounds of trumps, finishing in his own hand (!). Crossing to dummy with the Ace of diamonds, he successfully finessed the Jack of hearts. Then he cashed the Ace of hearts, dropping East's Queen.

"My partner had now, as they say, reached the crossroads. The contract was guaranteed (he could count on five trump tricks, three hearts and four top cards in the minor suits), but the overtrick hinged on guessing the heart position. Had East started life with the doubleton Queen? Or did he have Q-10-4 initially, in which case, the false card of the Queen would have been mandatory on the second round? As this was a pairs event, the overtrick was of course vital, and my partner spent a good deal of time pondering his choice. In the end, he played a heart to the King, hoping to drop the 10, and made only 12 tricks.

"'Sorry, partner,' he said, and explained that if he had taken the finesse against the 10—and it had failed—he would have gone down in six spades, having no further entry to dummy. At this point, I gave him my Bols Bridge Tip (or rather, part of it): *Count the opponents' hands!*

"He should have won the third round of trumps in dummy and then taken the heart finesse. With 12 tricks in the bag, he could now set about obtaining the vital count by playing three rounds of diamonds, ruffing the third round. The King of clubs comes next, the play to this trick revealing West's distribution: two spades, six diamonds, one club, and therefore, four hearts. Declarer can finesse dummy's 9 of hearts for a certain overtrick and a much better score on the board.

"Now we come to the second half of my Bols Tip, and it, too, has a story behind it. I was recently playing rubber bridge with my wife, who sometimes accuses me with considerable emotion (but, in my opinion, very little justification) of taking a superior attitude to her at the table. In consequence, she says, I fail to concentrate fully—and here she may be nearer the truth, as the reader may judge from a hand I played that evening in 6NT.

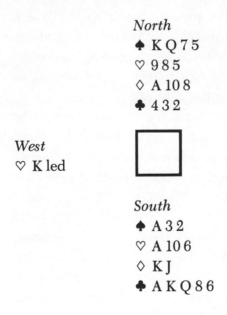

North
♠ K Q 7 5
♡ 9 8 5
◊ A 10 8
♣ 4 3 2

West
♡ K led

South
♠ A 3 2
♡ A 10 6
◊ K J
♣ A K Q 8 6

"West, who had opened the bidding with three hearts, led the King of hearts. East discarded a diamond, and I won with the Ace, continuing with five rounds of clubs."

With 11 tricks on top, assuming that the clubs will break, you might have expected the declarer to rectify the count for a squeeze by ducking the first round of hearts. Forquet doesn't comment on this, but if you look at the hand again, remembering that West has opened three hearts, you will see that a squeeze is most unlikely. The only menaces are in spades and diamonds, and the odds are East will control both these suits. As East sits over the dummy in both suits, you will never be able to squeeze him. Resuming the narrative:

"West and dummy each discarded two hearts on the long clubs, and East parted with two small diamonds. I cashed the Ace and King of spades and all followed.

"Now, I am a consistent fellow and follow the advice I give to others, so at this point, I applied the first part of my Bols Tip and began to count the opponents' hands. West had started with seven hearts, three clubs, and at least two spades. His 13th card was either a spade or a diamond. If it was a spade, the diamond finesse through East was a mathematical certainty; while if West held a diamond, the odds were 7 to 1 that his diamond was not the Queen. Armed with this analysis, I led a diamond from dummy, finessed the Jack . . . and went *down four*. This was the complete deal:

North
♠ K Q 7 5
♡ 9 8 5
◇ A 10 8
♣ 4 3 2

West
♠ 8 6
♡ K Q J 7 4 3 2
◇ Q
♣ J 9 7

East
♠ J 10 9 4
♡ —
◇ 9 7 6 5 4 3 2
♣ 10 5

South
♠ A 3 2
♡ A 10 6
◇ K J
♣ A K Q 8 6

"'Sorry, partner,' I said, trying to make the best of it. 'With the diamonds 7-1, you must admit I was unlucky to find the singleton Queen in West's hand.'

"'Down *four?*' said my wife.

"'Yeah, an unlucky hand,' I said, hoping she'd failed to notice my error. (Have you seen it?)

"'Wouldn't it have been better to end-play East with the fourth round of spades?' she asked.

"'Sure, I could have,' I replied. 'But it wouldn't have helped. If East held the Queen of diamonds, and exited with a low one, the suit would be blocked.' (I was beginning to realize she'd seen my mistake.)

"'Blocked? How can that be? I would have cashed the King of diamonds instead of taking that silly finesse. If West showed out, that would mean the spades were 3-3 and there would be 12 tricks on top. If West followed with a small diamond, I would simply cash the Queen of spades and lead dummy's last spade, discarding the Jack of diamonds on it. East would then have to lead into dummy's A-10 of diamonds at the end.'

"As you see, my wife was quite right, and it is to her that I am indebted for the completion of my tip:

"Count the opponents' hands—but when you have counted them, *play intelligently!*"

This was a good story, well told, though perhaps it had the form of a magazine article rather than a Bols Tip. My idea of this competition, though the adjudicators didn't always seem to agree, was that the reader should be able to say to himself, "Ah, yes, that's something I would not have thought of, but I will next time." For example, on the subject of obtaining a count of the opposing hands, there was an instructive point in a deal described by the Argentine international, Carlos Cabanne. It is necessary only to show the distribution of the club suit:

South was in four spades and West led the Jack of clubs, a suit that East had bid twice. The Jack was covered by the King and Ace, and East attacked a different suit. Later in the play, the declarer, to complete his count, had to decide whether the clubs were 7-1 or 6-2. (There had been no opportunity to test the suit by

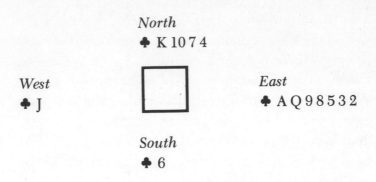

North

♣ K 10 7 4

West

♣ J

East

♣ A Q 9 8 5 3 2

South

♣ 6

ruffing a round.) The fact that East had not returned a club at trick two seemed a slight indication, and South played on the assumption of a 6-2 break, which turned out to be wrong.

Do you see what this is all about? The point is that Cabanne, the declarer, had no particular reason to cover the Jack of clubs at trick one. If he refrains from doing so, then West, if he has a second club, will doubtlessly lead it; if he does not, he can be read for a singleton. The conclusion is: don't prevent the opponents from revealing their distribution.

14. PIERRE JAIS (FRANCE)

"When you have not been able to show length in a suit on the first round, indicate the length of your remaining cards at the first opportunity."

In terms of international appearances, Pierre Jais, a Doctor of Medicine, is the longest-running star in Europe. He played in the first world championship in Budapest in 1937, a protege of the French master, Pierre Albarran. Since then, with Roger Trezel, he has won three world titles: the Bermuda Bowl in 1956, the Team Olympiad at Turin in 1960, and the Pairs Olympiad at Cannes in 1962. He played little serious bridge for a time after this, but reappeared with a new partner, Dominique Pilon, to win the European for France in 1969. France thus qualified for the 1971 Bermuda Bowl, where they were runners-up to the Aces.

In 1960, I adapted one of Jais's books into English, with the title, *How to Win at Rubber Bridge*. It was an interesting book, concentrating more on the mistakes that players make than on correct bidding. In my foreword, I wrote:

"Pierre Jais surveys the world from beneath hooded eyes with an abstracted air and a half smile and plays the sort of game you would expect from this book: thrustful, unpredictable, brilliant—yet sound. Since

131

France won the world championship of 1955 up to the great victory at Turin in 1960, Jais and Trezel have been regular members of the team. Pierre is quite amusing about this: 'After every championship they say we are too old and have played quite the worst of the three pairs. Then next year, they choose us first again.'"

Droll and irreverent, Pierre has not changed over the years. His tip is entitled, "Extend Your Suit-length Signals."

"My tip concerns the vital subject of signalling. You can effect quite an improvement in your defensive play by enlarging the use of suit-length signals to cover new situations.

"Practically everybody knows how to use suit-length signals on the first round of a suit: you play high-low to show an even number of cards, low-high to show an odd number. In this diagram, you are East and your partner leads the King of hearts:

North
♡ J 8 4

West
♡ K Q 9 7

East
♡ 6 5 3 2

South
♡ A 10

"On the lead of the King, you start an echo with the 5 or 6, showing an even number.

"So far, so good, but what happens when the cards are divided like this:

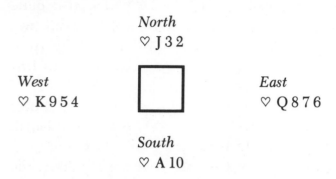

North
♡ J 3 2

West
♡ K 9 5 4

East
♡ Q 8 7 6

South
♡ A 10

"This time West leads the 4, dummy plays low, and your Queen loses to the Ace. Later, your partner gains the lead in another suit and lays down the King of hearts. In certain circumstances, it could be vital for West to know that South started with only two hearts. For example, if there is no outside entry to dummy, West will realize that he has two alternatives: to establish the fourth round or to switch to another suit, depriving the declarer of a second trick in hearts.

My suggestion

"My suggestion is that, as East, you should echo—or not echo—with your *remaining* cards in order to show how many you still have. In the above example, where East has three cards left in hearts, he should follow suit with the 6 on the second round. With Q-7-6 originally, East would follow with the 7 on the second round, starting an echo to show two cards remaining.

"The use of this signal enabled my partner to produce a nice defense in a recent match:

South dealer
Neither side vulnerable

                        North
                        ♠ K J 8 6 3
                        ♡ Q 10
                        ◊ J 4
                        ♣ J 10 4 2

West   *East*
♠ A 9 7 2   ♠ Q 10 5 4
♡ K 4   ♡ 8 7 3 2
◊ Q 6 5 3   ◊ K 8 7 2
♣ Q 8 7   ♣ 6

                        South
                        ♠ —
                        ♡ A J 9 6 5
                        ◊ A 10 9
                        ♣ A K 9 5 3

South	*North*
1♡	1♠
2♣	2♡
3♣	4♣
4♡	Pass

"West led the 3 of diamonds and my King lost to South's Ace. Declarer led a small heart toward the dummy, my partner winning with the King.

"My partner had good hopes of defeating the contract by taking one trick in each suit. The bidding had marked South with at least five hearts and five clubs. If South had two diamonds and one spade, the contract was sure to fail. However, if South had three diamonds and was void of spades, the defenders would have only three fast tricks and my partner would need to think again—which is just what he did.

"At the third trick, West led the Queen of diamonds and I played the 2. Declarer false-carded with the 10, but my partner, of course, decided to believe me. My play of the lowest diamond showed an odd number of cards remaining in the suit, and South was, therefore, known to have started with three diamonds. My partner now knew that the Ace of spades would be ruffed if he led it.

"West was able to judge, also, that I held four trumps, for apart from the use of a trump signal, it was easy to count the declarer for 0-5-3-5 distribution. Accordingly, West switched to the 2 of spades. He realized that if South misjudged the lie of the spade honors, he would lose control.

"And this is what happened. It seemed unlikely to the declarer that West would risk underleading the Ace of spades when South himself might (on the bidding) hold a singleton. So he finessed the Jack from dummy and was forced to ruff my Queen. South now needed all his trumps to draw mine, and when West eventually came in with the Queen of clubs, he was able to cash the Ace of spades for one down.

"My bridge tip is this: when you have not been able to signal length in a suit on the first round, indicate the length of your *remaining cards* at the first opportunity, whether following to the suit or discarding from it. You will find that this extra exchange of information will enable you to defeat many more contracts."

At the time when this piece was written, the fashion among British tournament players was to drop on the second round "the card you would have led from your original holding." For the most part, this produces the same answer as Jais's recommendation to play the lowest from an odd number, high-low from an even number. Thus, in both schemes, the second card from the diamond holding above, K-8-7-2, would be the 2. It seems to me, however, that when the original holding was three cards, such as Q-7-5, the Jais method would be clearer.

The situations that cause the greatest worry are those in a notrump contract where the leader needs to know on the first round how many cards of a suit his partner holds. Everyone is familiar with the uncertainty that can arise when you have led from a holding such as K-Q-9-x-x or K-Q-10-x:

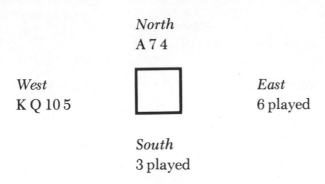

North
A 7 4

West
K Q 10 5

East
6 played

South
3 played

West leads the King, dummy plays low, East the 6, and South the 3. What is happening? It is hard to tell, because there are no universal conventions in this area. This is a similar situation:

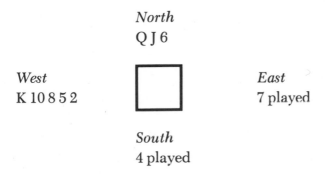

North
Q J 6

West
K 10 8 5 2

East
7 played

South
4 played

West leads the 5 at notrumps, dummy plays the Jack, East the 7, and South the 4. Of course, it is vital for West, if he is first to gain the lead, to know whether declarer started with A-x or A-x-x. On this occasion, is East showing a doubleton from 7-3, playing the lower card from 9-7, or making an encouraging gesture from

9-7-3-?. For all the modern talk about "attitude signals," you will find many different opinions.

In *Bridge for Tournament Players*, Albert Dormer
and I suggested that the best principle in defense was
for the second player to drop the *highest from three
low cards*. This was one of the examples we gave:

North
A 8

West   East
Q J 10 4 3   6 2

South
K 9 7 5

West leads the Queen, dummy plays the Ace, and
East the 2. West knows at once that East has a doubleton, because from 7-6-2 he would play the highest,
with 9-7-6-2 the second from the bottom. All methods
in this area work better on some hands than others, but
this play of the highest from x-x-x is usually clear, and
is the best counter to false-carding by the declarer.

The general subject of defensive signalling is
raised again in Dorothy Hayden Truscott's Bols Tip,
the first entry in the final year of the competition.

15. ANNA VALENTI (ITALY)

"Don't rush to draw trumps. On some hands you may be unable to draw them successfully; on others, even if you can draw them, you will be left with too few tricks."

The seventh and last entrant for the 2nd Bols Competition was one of Italy's leading woman players, Mrs. Anna Valenti. Although they have not yet succeeded in beating the Americans in the Venice Trophy (the feminine equivalent of the Bermuda Bowl), Italy's women have been nearly as dominant in European bridge as the men. In the early 1970s, they won four consecutive European Championships, as well as the 1972 and 1976 Team Olympiads. Like the men, they play fairly complicated bidding systems.

Anna Valenti has been a constant member of the national team. She learned to play bridge as a child and has played now for about 45 years. She and her husband enjoyed many successes together, including two Italian open team championships. In the women's team, her partner in recent years has been her sister-in-law, Marisa Bianchi, who herself is married to one of Italy's top players.

Mrs. Valenti has a highly competent, not to say formidable, presence at the bridge table and plays an aggressive game. Her tip is entitled, "Don't Rush to Draw Trumps:"

"When you have a trump suit divided 4-4, you should bear in mind that the outstanding trumps will break poorly (4-1 or 5-0) nearly one third of the time. If you cannot withstand such a division, you should give serious thought to playing out the hand without touching trumps.

"Provided you keep your head, you will be surprised how often this plan succeeds. Quite frequently you will find yourself making contracts that, to a bystander, would have seemed certain to fail.

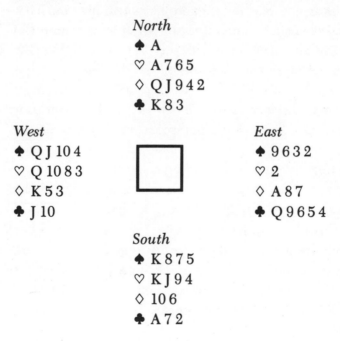

North
♠ A
♡ A 7 6 5
♦ Q J 9 4 2
♣ K 8 3

West
♠ Q J 10 4
♡ Q 10 8 3
♦ K 5 3
♣ J 10

East
♠ 9 6 3 2
♡ 2
♦ A 8 7
♣ Q 9 6 5 4

South
♠ K 8 7 5
♡ K J 9 4
♦ 10 6
♣ A 7 2

"You are in four hearts and West leads the Queen of spades. If you set about drawing trumps, you will surely lose two hearts and two diamonds, for one down.

"There is no great danger of an early overruff, and if the diamonds are going to break badly, you won't necessarily lose by playing them early on. So, the first move should be to lead, not a trump, but a low diamond from dummy. The 10 loses to the King and West shifts to the Jack of clubs. You win in hand and cash the King of spades, discarding a club from the table.

"A low spade is ruffed and you lead the Queen of diamonds from dummy. East wins and, observing that you have not seemed keen to play trumps yourself, leads his singleton heart, West's 8 forcing dummy's Ace. The position now is:

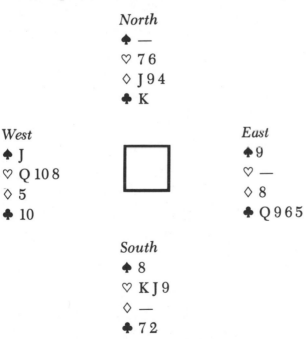

North
♠ —
♡ 7 6
♢ J 9 4
♣ K

West
♠ J
♡ Q 10 8
♢ 5
♣ 10

East
♠ 9
♡ —
♢ 8
♣ Q 9 6 5

South
♠ 8
♡ K J 9
♢ —
♣ 7 2

"Continuing to play on crossruff lines, you cash the King of clubs, ruff the Jack of diamonds, a winner, and ruff a spade. You refrain from ruffing the next lead and triumphantly make ♡ K-J at the finish."

I am not sure about this hand. It is slightly double-dummyish in the sense that, playing as suggested, you might run into an untimely ruff and lose a contract that would be laydown if trumps were 3-2. On the other hand, it is a fact that in hands of this type, good players do not—as a rule—meet the trump suit head on. It is generally right to test the side suit first because, if you do meet a bad break, the odds are that the player who ruffs will have long trumps. There are also many hands where you leave a defender with a trump because, if there is a ruff, the trick will come back.

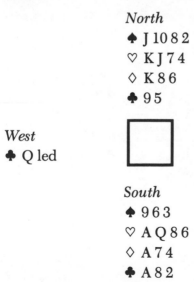

North
♠ J 10 8 2
♡ K J 7 4
◇ K 8 6
♣ 9 5

West
♣ Q led

South
♠ 9 6 3
♡ A Q 8 6
◇ A 7 4
♣ A 8 2

Playing in two hearts, you win the club lead, and draw two rounds of trumps before starting the spades. If all goes well, you make an overtrick: if there is a spade ruff, you still make the contract. Drawing the last trump would not help, as then the opponents would come to a diamond trick. Mrs. Valenti continues:

"Whenever there is danger of losing too many trump tricks, you should hesitate to launch a frontal assault on the trump suit. This is especially so when there has been competitive bidding, for a favorable break in trumps is then less likely.

North
♠ A J 7 5
♡ 10 7 3
♢ A 4
♣ A 7 6 2

West
♠ 6
♡ A K 8 6
♢ 10 8 7
♣ K Q 10 9 8

East
♠ Q 10 9 8
♡ 9 4 2
♢ 9 6 5
♣ 5 4 3

South
♠ K 4 3 2
♡ Q J 5
♢ K Q J 3 2
♣ J

"You play in four spades after West has overcalled in clubs. West begins with the Ace of hearts and switches to the King of clubs.

"Because the diamonds are more or less solid, it is tempting to draw trumps. However, you lose nothing by beginning with a club ruff and setting out to establish your trick in hearts by advancing the Queen. (This is safe, because if the opponents could ruff a heart, they would have done so.) If West returns a third club, you ruff, cash the heart winner, and cross to the Ace of diamonds to lead dummy's last club.

"Suppose that East discards a diamond. You ruff and cash the King of spades and a second diamond. You have won eight tricks, the defenders two. You ruff the next diamond with a low trump and East is end-played.

"If East elects to ruff the fourth round of clubs, you overruff, cash two diamonds, and end-play East as before.

"Even when your trump suit is solid, it may still be fatal to touch this suit too early. The next example is one of my favorite hands.

"South was in four spades and West led the Queen of clubs, won by dummy's King. South's first move was to lead a diamond, establishing communications, rather than to test the trumps. West continued with the 10 of clubs and East ruffed. East correctly returned a trump and West showed out, dummy winning with the 8.

North
- ♠ K Q J 8
- ♡ A
- ◇ 10 9 7 5 3
- ♣ K 6 4

West
- ♠ —
- ♡ K 7 3 2
- ◇ A K 8 2
- ♣ Q J 10 7 3

East
- ♠ 10 6 5 4 2
- ♡ 10 9 5 4
- ◇ J 6 4
- ♣ 2

South
- ♠ A 9 7 3
- ♡ Q J 8 6
- ◇ Q
- ♣ A 9 8 5

"After this unfavorable development, declarer saw that she would need a second trick in hearts. The Ace of hearts was cashed, and the closed hand was entered with a diamond ruff. The Queen of hearts was covered by the King and ruffed in dummy. After another diamond ruff, the Jack of hearts was cashed and the fourth heart was ruffed. South had taken eight tricks and still had a high trump in each hand.

"If South had taken even one round of trumps early on, East would have been able to play a second trump when he ruffed the club, leaving South with only nine winners.

"My bridge tip is this: don't rush to draw trumps. On some hands you may be unable to draw them successfully; on others, even if you can draw them, you may find that you are left with too few tricks. On all such hands, you should consider whether it may be better to make as many tricks as you can by crossruffing."

This was an interesting study of one of the "gray" areas of card-play. You wouldn't find any of these hands in a textbook as examples of when to draw trumps or of when not to draw trumps. There is no doubt that an average player would go down on all three hands, and it wouldn't be easy to convince him that he had made any sort of mistake.

Players learning the game are taught to extract a losing trump against them, but this play is very often unnecessary and sometimes a definite mistake. It is sufficient simply to observe a four-card ending of this sort:

Diamonds are trumps, South needs three of the last four tricks, and we will assume that he knows more or less how the cards lie. It is clear that if he draws the trump against him, he will make only the King of clubs afterwards. If the lead were in dummy, he might think of leading the Queen of hearts, in an attempt to pin the 8; this would be good enough if West held ♡ 8 instead of ♡ 3. But a club to the King always wins. East must ruff and must concede another trick with his next lead. It is because of this kind of possibility that good players often refrain from drawing the last trump against them, to the consternation of less expert partners.

North
- ♠ —
- ♡ Q 6
- ♢ 10
- ♣ K

West
- ♠ J
- ♡ 3
- ♢ —
- ♣ 10 8

East
- ♠ —
- ♡ K 8 2
- ♢ 4
- ♣ —

South
- ♠ 7
- ♡ —
- ♢ J
- ♣ 5 3

THE AWARDS FOR
BRIDGE TIPS 9 TO 15

A panel of 28 experts from 22 countries adjudicated the seven entries for the second competition. To remind you, the entries were:

1. HOWARD SCHENKEN: *When on defense in third position, cultivate the habit of playing slowly to the first trick.*

2. JEREMY FLINT: *Instead of stolidly pushing out an unimaginative small card from three or four to an honor, you should consider whether to lead the honor.*

3. JIM JACOBY: *When a good opponent seemingly gives you a present—stay alert! Watch for a trap. Beware bridge players bearing gifts!*

4. JEAN BESSE: *Beware of your trump tricks. When you see a chance for an easy overruff, don't be in too much of a hurry to take it.*

5. PIETRO FORQUET: *Count the opponents' hands—but when you have counted them, play intelligently.*

6. PIERRE JAIS: *When you have not been able to show length in a suit on the first round, indicate the length of your remaining cards at the first opportunity.*

7. ANNA VALENTI: *Don't rush to draw trumps. On some hands, you may be unable to draw them successfully; on others, even if you could draw them, you will be left with too few tricks.*

Where would your choice have fallen? On Schenken's warning to think things out when in third position? On Flint's reminder that it is sometimes right to lead high from three or four to an honor? On Jacoby's advice to look twice at Greek gifts? Besse's description of the dangers of over-ruffing? Forquet's elegant tale about the failure to play intelligently after counting the opponents' hands? The signalling system proposed by Jais? Or Anna Valenti's warning not to be in a rush to draw trumps?

Well, it was fairly certain that Jean Besse's article, both instructive and providing excellent column material, would receive high marks. The maximum was 560 points and the scores for the first three were:

1. *Jean Besse* (dangers of overruffing), 472 points.

2. *Howard Schenken* (take your time at trick one), 429 points.

3. *Pietro Forquet* (play intelligently), 428 points.

It seems to me, that in making the second and third awards, the judges gave more weight to "column material" than to instructional value. I mean, "take your time in third position" and "play intelligently when you have the count" are estimable pieces of advice, but are they really Bridge Tips that a player can put in his locker?

If you adopt the other standard—that of providing a memorable tip in a specialized area—then some of the other entries deserved a prize. If I were to mention one, it would be Jeremy Flint's tip about leading high from three or four to an honor in certain circumstances.

16. DOROTHY HAYDEN TRUSCOTT (U.S.A.)

"Against notrumps, defender's first spot card, unless it is essential to give the count, should indicate attitude to the opening leader's suit."

The former Dorothy Hayden is married to Alan Truscott, who once represented Britain in the Bermuda Bowl and is now bridge columnist of the New York Times. Mrs. Truscott has the unique record of having represented her country in all four forms of major competition: Bermuda Bowl, Venice Trophy, Olympiad Pairs, and Olympiad Teams. Only one other woman has played in the Bermuda Bowl. In the three contests for the Venice Trophy, Mrs. Truscott has been on the winning side each time, once against Britain, twice against Italy. Her wins in ACBL tournaments include the Blue Ribbon Pairs and the Lifemaster Pairs.

As Dorothy Hayden, she is the author of two books, *Bid Better, Play Better* and *Winning Declarer Play*, the second of which has been published in Britain by Robert Hale.

Of the outstanding woman players, some are essentially "flair" players, possessing exceptional card sense; Rixi Markus, Fritzi Gordon, and the late Helen Sobel belong to that category. Others have worked hard at the game and have developed a sound technique. Mrs. Truscott, I would say, stands somewhere between the two—a mathematician with a first-class mind that could have been applied with equal success to any intellectual pastime. Her tip is concerned with defensive signalling and is entitled "Show Attitude to the Opening Leader's Suit":

"The last major innovation in signalling came 40 years ago, when suit preference signals were introduced. But in all that time, there has been a serious gap in the signalling methods available to the defenders. My tip, a modification of a suggestion by T.R.H. Lyons, of England, is an attempt to fill that gap.

"Suppose West leads the spade 4 against 3NT and sees this:

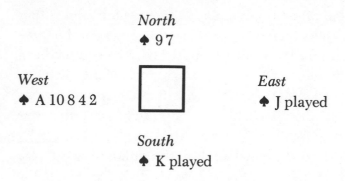

North
♠ 9 7

West
♠ A 10 8 4 2

East
♠ J played

South
♠ K played

"Dummy plays the 7, East the Jack, and declarer the King. Who has the Queen? West can't tell. If he gets the lead in some other suit, should he try to cash his spades or should he wait for partner to lead the suit?

"My Bols Tip is this: against notrumps, defender's first spot card, unless it is essential to give count, should indicate attitude toward the opening leader's suit.

North
♠ 9 7
♡ Q 10 2
◇ 7 6 5 4
♣ A K Q J

West
♠ A 10 8 4 2
♡ 9 8 7
◇ K 3
♣ 9 7 3

East
♠ Q J 5
♡ K J 6 4
◇ 10 9 8
♣ 10 8 2

South
♠ K 6 3
♡ A 5 3
◇ A Q J 2
♣ 6 5 4

South	*North*
1◇	2♣
2NT	3NT

"West leads the 4 of spades against 3NT. Declarer wins East's Jack with the King, and leads a club to dummy. East should play the 10 of clubs on this trick, meaning: 'I love your lead, partner. Please continue.'

(Notice that it would be virtually useless for East to give his partner the count in the club suit here.) Declarer takes the diamond finesse, and when West wins the King, he cashes four spade tricks, for one down.

"Now, suppose that the East and South cards had been slightly different:

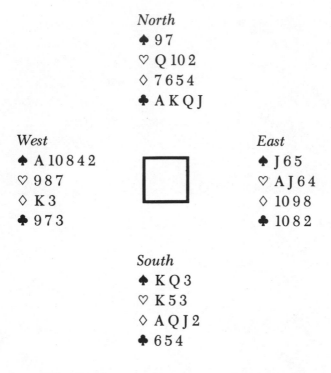

North
♠ 9 7
♡ Q 10 2
◊ 7 6 5 4
♣ A K Q J

West
♠ A 10 8 4 2
♡ 9 8 7
◊ K 3
♣ 9 7 3

East
♠ J 6 5
♡ A J 6 4
◊ 10 9 8
♣ 10 8 2

South
♠ K Q 3
♡ K 5 3
◊ A Q J 2
♣ 6 5 4

"The bidding is the same and West, who has the same hand as before, makes the same opening lead and sees the same dummy. Again, declarer wins the Jack of spades with the King, and leads a club. This time, however, East cannot stand a spade continuation from partner, so he contributes the 2 of clubs.

"Declarer takes a diamond finesse, losing to the King. West now knows that he can't afford to continue spades from his side of the table, and he exits with the 9 of hearts. East grabs the trick, returns the 6 of spades, and the contract fails by two tricks.

"Note that in both these cases, West would have been on a complete guess without the 'attitude' signal. And if he had guessed wrong, declarer would have made both games."

"Complete guess" puts it a bit high, I think. Most players would scramble out of the first dilemma, at any rate, by some energetic suit-preference signalling. Holding the spade Jack, East would play the 10 of clubs on the first round of clubs and the 10 of diamonds on the first round of diamonds. On some occasions, of course, there would be less scope for suit-preference, though the whole discussion contains the implication that the defender has a choice. Mrs. Truscott continues:

"The opening leader should also use the same attitude signal. In the situations already given, he should play the 9 of clubs on the second trick to emphasize that he wants the suit to be continued. But sometimes West will want to discourage partner from pursuing the suit originally led:

"West elects to lead the 4 of hearts against 3NT. Declarer takes East's Queen with the King, and tries a diamond finesse. If West wanted hearts to be returned,

North
♠ 5 4 3 2
♡ 9
♢ A Q J 10 7
♣ A J 4

West
♠ A Q 10 6
♡ J 8 6 4 2
♢ 9 6 2
♣ 5

East
♠ J 9 8
♡ Q 10 5 3
♢ K 3
♣ 8 7 6 3

South
♠ K 7
♡ A K 7
♢ 8 5 4
♣ K Q 10 9 2

South	West	North	East
—	—	1♢	Pass
2♣	Pass	2♢	Pass
3NT	Pass	Pass	Pass

he would play the diamond 9 on this trick. If he were lukewarm about the matter, he might play the 6.

"With his actual hand, however, West is most anxious for a shift and should play the 2. East wins with the King and can beat the contract with a spade shift. If he blindly continues hearts, declarer will make 11 tricks."

Mrs. Truscott's tip led to a certain amount of agitated correspondence. Dealing rather gingerly with the matter in a subsequent edition of the *IBPA Bulletin*, the editor, Albert Dormer, wrote:

"Mrs. Truscott described her tip as: '. . . a modification of a suggestion by T.R.H. Lyons of England. . . .' It is indeed true that Mrs. Truscott's suggestion was prompted by an article written by Flt. Lt. Lyons—an Air Force officer serving abroad—and he is to be congratulated on having conceived this idea. But the fact is that the idea is not new.

"Under the title, 'A New Signal for Defenders,' Mr. I.G. Smith put forward a virtually identical scheme of signalling with detailed examples in the December 1963 issue of the *British Bridge World.*"

In other words, the idea of a signal relating to a declarer's attitude to the suit led against notrumps has been around for some time—not that this was any reason why the notion should not be developed in the course of a Bols Tip. The basic idea of the Smith Peters was that a peter in the first suit played by the declarer should signify undisclosed values in the suit led by partner; but the opening leader himself used the peter only to *deter* his partner from returning the first suit. Mr. Smith's original article also drew attention to other occasions where this kind of information is vital to the defenders, such as:

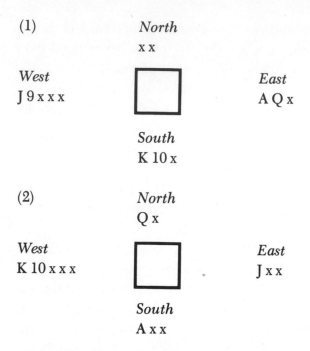

(1)

North
x x

West
J 9 x x x

East
A Q x

South
K 10 x

(2)

North
Q x

West
K 10 x x x

East
J x x

South
A x x

In (1), East correctly plays the Queen on the first round and South wins with the King. The defense will go wrong unless West is able to read the position. In (2), after dummy's Queen has been played, East will drop his middle card, but West may still not be confident about the Jack.

Dormer and I once proposed yet another scheme of this nature, called the "Oddball." (Probably someone else thought of that, too!) The idea was that any irregular play by either defender, such as an echo with three cards or the meaningless play of an honor card, should constitute an endorsement of the suit originally led. Thus, if you wish to compare the alternative ideas:

To advise continuation of the first suit led:

	Leader plays	Leader's partner plays
SMITH:	not a peter	a peter
LYONS- TRUSCOTT:	unnecessarily high card	unnecessarily high card
ODDBALL:	any irregular card	any irregular card

The Italian idea, which in Britain we call (rightly or wrongly) "Busso," is also worth noting. This involves "attitude" leads. The principle is that the lower the card led, the stronger the suggestion that the future of the defense appears to lie in this suit. Remember the West hand in Mrs. Truscott's third example:

♠ A Q 10 6
♡ J 8 6 4 2
◊ 9 6 2
♣ 3

Playing Busso, you would lead the 6 of hearts, immediately conveying to your partner that you had prospects apart from the suit led. Had the hearts been A-J-8-6-2 and the spades A-x-x-x, you would have led ♡ 2. With a long but not strong suit, such as K-9-7-5-3-2, you might lead the 3, reserving the option later to discard the 5 (meaning that you still favored this suit) or the 2 (meaning that a switch would be considered).

When none of these methods is in use, it may be possible to flash the vital message, not through a conventional signal, but by inviting partner to use his brains. A sparkling play suggested by Peter Swinnerton-Dyer (now Sir Peter, the 17th baronet and Master of St. Catherine's College, Cambridge), stays in the mind.

```
                     North
                     ♠ K 9 5
                     ♡ A K Q J 5
                     ◊ Q J 6
                     ♣ 10 5

West                                      East
♠ Q J 6 4 2          ┌─────────┐          ♠ 7 3
♡ 10 2               │         │          ♡ 9 7 6
◊ K 10 2             │         │          ◊ A 9 7 4
♣ A Q 9             └─────────┘          ♣ J 7 4 3

                     South
                     ♠ A 10 8
                     ♡ 8 4 3
                     ◊ 8 5 3
                     ♣ K 8 6 2
```

South	West	North	East
Pass	1♠	Dble	Pass
1NT	Pass	2NT	Pass
3NT	Pass	Pass	Pass

West led the 4 of spades and declarer won with the 10, returning a diamond. Dummy's Jack was taken by East who continued spades. Now South was able to establish a diamond for nine tricks.

Peter, who was West, blamed himself. Declarer can be counted for eight tricks in the major suits. On the first diamond, West must go in with the King and exit with a heart! The abandonment of spades tells East that only a club switch holds hope, and his subsequent lead of the Jack defeats the contract.

17. PER-OLOV SUNDELIN (SWEDEN)

"If you can't see yourself beating the contract by winning the trick, DUCK IT —even at the cost of a trick."

Per-Olov Sundelin is one of the personable young Swedes—well, young as bridge players go—who have brought their country to the front rank, reviving the days when Kock-Werner, Lilliehook-Anulf and, later, Wohlin, were the best in Europe. Having knocked on the door several times, Sweden won the 1978 European Championship in Denmark by a clear margin. The team was disappointed by its performance in the Bermuda Bowl later, where it finished third to the U.S.A. and Italy.

Sundelin has represented his country consistently since 1963, captaining the team in 1972 and 1973. He has achieved fine results in the Pairs Olympiad, the Teams Olympiad, and the Sunday Times International Pairs.

A systems analyst by profession, Per-Olov is a great "party man" and speaks English so well that he makes clever puns in the language! The deals he describes below are not inventions—they represent his own experiences in the Monte Carlo Olympiad. His tip, which begins on similar lines to that of Charles Goren in the first series, is entitled "Be Bold When You Are Defending."

"You are all familiar with the situation where you sit over dummy's K-Q-10 with A-x-x. When declarer leads up to the King, you smoothly play low. On the next round, declarer may go wrong, and at least you have spread uncertainty.

"Some of you have even fooled declarer by ducking with the King when sitting over A-Q-J-x-x. Perhaps the declarer then wasted an entry, or released a guard, to enter his hand for another finesse. Such plays are still more effective when the defender sits over the closed hand.

"These are valuable—indeed, essential—stratagems. But they are seldom very risky or unexpected. In this field, you haven't really arrived until you are willing actually to sacrifice a winner: you must be prepared deliberately to give away a trick for the possibility of leading declarer astray.

"This type of play is exclusively for the bold and courageous. In this hand you are East:

South	West	North	East
1♡	1♠	2♢	Pass
3♣	Pass	4♡	Pass
Pass	Pass		

"West leads the Queen of spades. South's problem is to take care of his losers in the black suits. The opposition bidding makes ruffing look risky, so declarer naturally thinks about the diamond finesse. If the Jack loses to the King, it should still be possible to hold the trump losers to two.

South dealer
East-West vulnerable

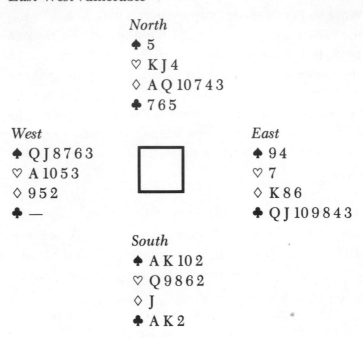

North
- ♠ 5
- ♡ K J 4
- ◊ A Q 10 7 4 3
- ♣ 7 6 5

West
- ♠ Q J 8 7 6 3
- ♡ A 10 5 3
- ◊ 9 5 2
- ♣ —

East
- ♠ 9 4
- ♡ 7
- ◊ K 8 6
- ♣ Q J 10 9 8 4 3

South
- ♠ A K 10 2
- ♡ Q 9 8 6 2
- ◊ J
- ♣ A K 2

"As East, you ought to have a perfect picture of the hands. In view of his three club bid, South is marked with three to the Ace-King. He must also hold the Ace and King of spades and, since West did not pre-empt, one or two low spades as well. The odds, therefore, are that his hearts are headed by the Queen; at any rate, you must assume this.

"To resume: South wins the first trick with the Ace and leads the Jack of diamonds. West plays the 2, showing an odd number, and dummy the 3. Your count is confirmed. You decide, quickly and without a flicker, that declarer will wrap up 10 tricks quite easily if you play the obvious defense of winning with the King and giving your partner a club ruff.

"So you duck. You don't know what will happen next, but you do know that, with normal defense, the declarer would make his contract.

"South now plays a trump to the Jack and cashes the Ace of diamonds, shedding a spade. The postion is:

North
♠ —
♡ K 4
◊ Q 10 7 4
♣ 7 6 5

West
♠ J 8 7 6 3
♡ A 10 5
◊ 9
♣ —

East
♠ 9
♡ —
◊ K
♣ Q J 10 9 8 4 3

South
♠ K 10
♡ Q 9 8 6
◊ —
♣ A K 2

"South wants to enter his hand for a spade ruff. As the cards lie, he can play a diamond, but he may be afraid that East will discard a spade on this trick. So South is quite likely to try a club—which turns out to be fatal when West ruffs and continues with Ace and another trump.

"In my second deal, South plays in three spades and again you are East.

East dealer
Neither side vulnerable

North
♠ 8 5 3
♡ 10
♢ K J 5 2
♣ A Q 10 8 3

West
♠ Q 7
♡ Q 9 2
♢ Q 10 9 7 6
♣ 7 5 2

East
♠ 10 6 2
♡ A K 8 4 3
♢ A
♣ K 9 6 4

South
♠ A K J 9 4
♡ J 7 6 5
♢ 8 4 3
♣ J

South	West	North	East
—	—	—	1♡
1♠	2♡	3♡	Dble
3♠	Pass	Pass	Pass

"North's bid of three hearts is an 'unassuming cue bid,' signifying a sound raise to three spades.

"West leads the 2 of hearts to his partner's King and East returns a trump, won by the Ace. Deciding that a crossruff is unlikely to produce more than eight tricks, South runs the Jack of clubs. If the finesse loses, he will still have chances.

"As East, have you tried to plan ahead? What is declarer's hand? You know he has five spades to the A-K-Q or A-K-J, and you place him with four hearts, because your style of defense is to lead third best from an honor combination. When you see partner's 2 of clubs, the count is complete. (If partner had held a singleton club, he would have led it; also, with three clubs, South would have played differently.)

"It is easy to see that if you take the club and return a trump, South will go up with the King, ruff a heart and play clubs, probably ending up with an overtrick.

"Now see what happens when you duck the club lead. South is sure to go for a crossruff, because he will think it safe to ruff clubs until the King appears. Four tricks later, the position will be:

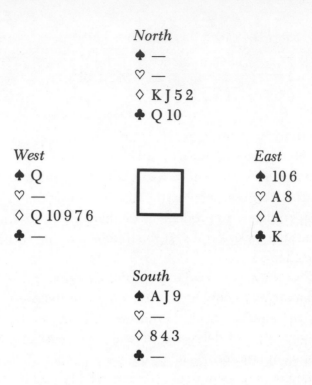

North
♠ —
♡ —
◇ K J 5 2
♣ Q 10

West
♠ Q
♡ —
◇ Q 10 9 7 6
♣ —

East
♠ 10 6
♡ A 8
◇ A
♣ K

South
♠ A J 9
♡ —
◇ 8 4 3
♣ —

"Astonishment spreads over declarer's face when dummy's club is covered by your King. Whatever he does, he is defeated. If South ruffs, West overruffs, and puts you in with the diamond Ace, you continue hearts and your 10 of spades becomes the setting trick.

"Once again, boldness pays dividends: if you can't gain by winning, DUCK!"

Players are nervous of ducking when they can see that their King, Queen, or even Ace, may never make, but the trick almost always comes back. Suppose a side suit is divided in this way:

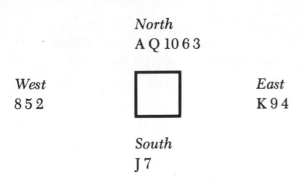

North
A Q 10 6 3

West
8 5 2

East
K 9 4

South
J 7

South finesses the Jack and East, seeing his partner's 2, is afraid to hold up his King. But even supposing the declarer goes up with the Ace on the next round and then ruffs the King, as a rule nothing will be lost: declarer will make four winners in the suit either way.

Sundelin's second deal illustrates one of the most important principles in defense: be very reluctant to release a control in an important side suit. Suppose a suit is divided in this way:

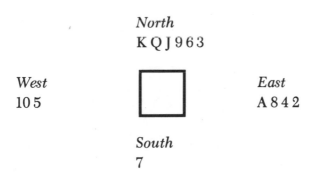

North
K Q J 9 6 3

West
10 5

East
A 8 4 2

South
7

When South leads to the King, you may create havoc by ducking. Declarer will follow with the

Queen, then play a third round and ruff low, expecting the Ace to fall from West. Instead, West will overruff and the suit will still not be established. If the worst happens—if the contract is made and you find you could have defeated it by taking your top tricks—you can be sure that your partner will appreciate your good intentions!

18. TONY PRIDAY (ENGLAND)

"When you are defending, remember the art of camouflage. If you can mislead the declarer in one suit, he may well jump to a wrong conclusion in another suit."

Tony Priday first represented Britain at Torquay in 1961, partnered by Alan Truscott and winning the European Championship. He was concerned then in one of the most famous deals of all time: he declined (for a good reason) to lead an Ace against a grand slam, and was later squeezed out of it.

In recent years, Priday and Rodrigue have been the backbone of every British team, and in the Miami Olympiad, especially, Priday was the outstanding player.

Tony manages his family's long-established timber business and, on arriving at a hotel, never fails to comment on the quality and commercial source of the woodwork. Because of business ties, he cannot very well spare the time to play in world pairs events, but he has an excellent record in the *Sunday Times* and, in 1979, won the open pairs at Marbella against some of the strongest competition in Europe. Tony and his wife, Jane, are an outstanding combination, Jane having won two world titles.

A Wykehamist, Tony embodies the precept of the Founder, "Manners Makyth Man." Sorry if you've heard it before, but everyone likes the story of the two elderly ladies in a hotel lounge at Torquay, one of them saying to the other:

"That was Mr. Priday; such a nice gentleman."

"Oh, I agree with you, dear. I was so surprised to learn he was one of the bridge players."

Tony's bridge tip is entitled "When you are defending, practice the art of camouflage:"

"Military men give much thought to camouflage. Thus a general, when planning a defensive battle, will pretend to be strong in a part of the line where he is weak. He will also seek to appear vulnerable in a place where he is strong.

"Defenders at bridge have many opportunities to do the same. When you are strong in a suit, you aim to conceal the fact. There is then a good chance that declarer will misread your strength in another—and perhaps vital—suit.

"This hand was played in the home international series between England and Northern Ireland:

"When England was East-West, the bidding went:

South	West	North	East
—	—	—	1♠
Pass	2♠	Dble	Pass
3♣	Pass	4NT	Pass
5♣	Pass	Pass	Pass

East dealer
Both sides vulnerable

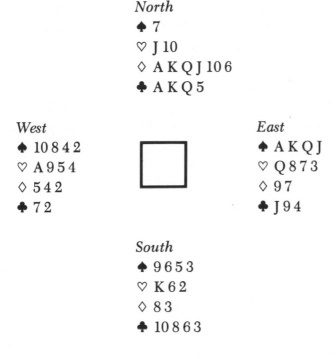

North
♠ 7
♡ J 10
◊ A K Q J 10 6
♣ A K Q 5

West
♠ 10 8 4 2
♡ A 9 5 4
◊ 5 4 2
♣ 7 2

East
♠ A K Q J
♡ Q 8 7 3
◊ 9 7
♣ J 9 4

South
♠ 9 6 5 3
♡ K 6 2
◊ 8 3
♣ 10 8 6 3

"North jumped to 4NT because there would be a good chance for six clubs if partner held an Ace. If the Ace of hearts, no problem; if the Ace of spades, West might still lead a spade.

"As it was, West led the 2 of spades against five clubs. East could see at once that the defense would need to win two heart tricks. If East won with the Jack of spades, South would place West with the Ace of hearts, for his raise to two spades. So East won with the *Ace* of spades and returned a low heart. Placing West with the King of spades (at least), and therefore, East with the Ace of hearts, South rose with the King and was defeated.

"In that example, camouflage took the form of concealing the strength in one suit (spades) to simulate strength in another (hearts). It is often possible to do the opposite. Here you are East and declarer leads low from dummy:

North
x x x

West　　　　　　　　　　　　*East*
A x x x　　　　　　　　　　　K x x

South
Q J x

"You cannot, of course, prevent declarer from establishing a trick in this suit. But if you make the bold play of putting up the King when a low card is led from the table, declarer may place you with A-K, and this may cause him to misread the lie in another suit. A defender used this stratagem effectively on the following deal:

"You may not approve of North's bidding, but this is the way it went in the final stages of Britain's Gold Cup some years ago.

"West led the Ace of diamonds and, when his partner encouraged with the 7, continued with ◊ 3. East

South dealer
Both sides vulnerable

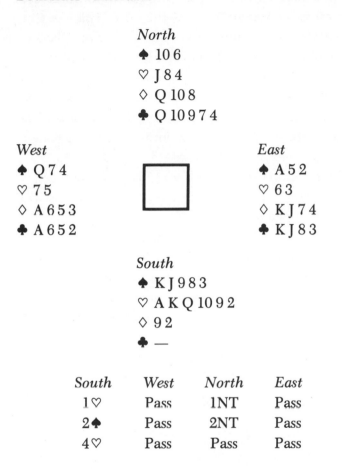

North
♠ 10 6
♡ J 8 4
◇ Q 10 8
♣ Q 10 9 7 4

West
♠ Q 7 4
♡ 7 5
◇ A 6 5 3
♣ A 6 5 2

East
♠ A 5 2
♡ 6 3
◇ K J 7 4
♣ K J 8 3

South
♠ K J 9 8 3
♡ A K Q 10 9 2
◇ 9 2
♣ —

South	West	North	East
1♡	Pass	1NT	Pass
2♠	Pass	2NT	Pass
4♡	Pass	Pass	Pass

took the second trick with the Jack and realized that South's distribution was almost certainly 5-6-2-0. In that case, the contract might well hinge on a guess in spades. East therefore set out to camouflage his spade holding.

"At the third trick, East laid down the King of clubs! Declarer ruffed with a high trump and entered dummy with a heart to lead the 10 of spades. Convinced that East must hold the club Ace, declarer placed West with the Ace of spades and so ran the 10, losing to the Queen.

"My bridge tip is this: when you are defending, remember the art of camouflage. If you can mislead declarer in one suit, he may well jump to a wrong conclusion in another suit."

This was an advanced lesson for tournament players, covering an area where there are many opportunities for imaginative play.

There are various ways in which defenders can mislead the declarer about distribution as well as about high cards. Most players understand the general principle of "playing the card you are known to hold." This is often important when declarer threatens to ruff out a suit.

> *North*
> A Q 9 5 2
>
> *West*   □   *East*
> K J 8   10 4 3
>
> *South*
> 7 6

South leads the 6 to the Queen and follows with the Ace. West must not fail now to drop the King, the card he is known to hold. South will not necessarily be misled, but he will be uncertain whether it is safe to continue the suit and ruff low on the next round. The play of the King would also be right if West had K-J-8-x.

Sometimes it is good play to part with a master card to mislead a declarer who is trying to discover the distribution:

South dealer
Neither side vulnerable

North
♠ K 7 5 4
♡ J 5 3 2
◊ A 8 4
♣ 7 2

West
♠ Q 9
♡ A K Q 6
◊ Q 9 7 2
♣ 10 8 5

East
♠ 10 3
♡ 9 8 4
◊ K 10 6 3
♣ Q 9 6 3

South
♠ A J 8 6 2
♡ 10 7
◊ J 5
♣ A K J 4

South	West	North	East
1♠	Pass	2♠	Pass
Pass	Dble	3♠	Pass
4♠	Pass	Pass	Pass

West began with two top hearts, then switched to
◇ 2. South led this run to East's King, and East returned the 6 of clubs to declarer's Ace.

Instead of taking an early view about the trump
distribution, South took a ruff in diamonds, cashed
♠ K, and returned to ♣ K. The position was now:

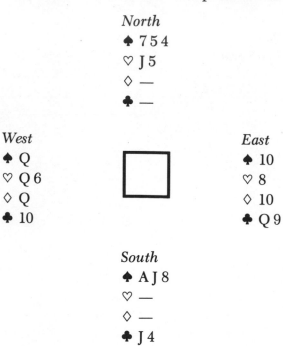

North
♠ 7 5 4
♡ J 5
◇ —
♣ —

West
♠ Q
♡ Q 6
◇ Q
♣ 10

East
♠ 10
♡ 8
◇ 10
♣ Q 9

South
♠ A J 8
♡ —
◇ —
♣ J 4

When South, still on his tour of inspection, ruffed a
low club, East followed with the *Queen*. Falling victim
to his own curiosity, South placed West with 1-4-4-4
distribution and finessed the Jack of spades.

19. BENITO GAROZZO (ITALY)

"Games may be quietly defended, but slams must be ATTACKED.*"*

Benito Garozzo developed his game after the war in Egypt. ("In those days *I* was the big expert," Leon Yallouze once told me with a smile.) In 1957, Benito played a tournament in London with D'Alelio. He played in his first world championship in 1961 and, from then on, was unbeaten in Bermuda Bowl and Team Olympiad competitions until 1976.

Garozzo and Forquet were an unbreakable rock in match play, and whenever Garozzo was teamed with Belladonna in one of the big pairs events, the only question, in Walter Hagen's phrase, was "Who'll be second?"

Benito has a jewelry business in Rome, with contacts in America. Dark, on the short side, he stands with his shoulders back, wavy black hair curving away from an impressive forehead and spectacles. Away from the table, he is the most polite and unassuming of men, but with 13 cards in his hand he becomes a demon, his brain never resting from attempts to cause alarm and uncertainty.

Doing the commentary on Vu-Graph for the 1978 European Championship in Denmark, I saw a good deal of his partnership with Arturo Franco. Benito, I realized, was not an overbidder, but above all a "pressure" player, constantly involving his opponents in difficult decisions. His Bols Tip, characteristically, is entitled "Against a Slam Contract, ATTACK!"

"Heroic measures are rarely needed when leading against a game contract. The defenders can expect to get the lead again after the dummy has been exposed, and the early play offers further clues to what they should do.

"Not so against slams. Unless two tricks can be cashed at once, the defense must strike a telling blow to develop the setting trick by the opening lead. Later is too late.

"The one factor that works in favor of the defense is that declarer is rarely willing to risk immediate defeat if any alternative seems attractive. And sometimes such an alternative can be created by the lead itself. For example, your opponents have bid to six diamonds as follows:

South	North
—	1♣
2◊	3♣
3◊	3♠
4NT	5♡
5NT	6◊
Pass	

"Sitting West, you hold:

♠ Q 9 5 2
♡ K 8 4
◊ J 5 3 2
♣ K J

"In most ways, your defensive prospects are poor. The K-J of clubs look dead, underneath the rebid suit, and the King of hearts is unlikely to take a trick. But do not despair: you have one asset the declarer knows nothing about—your trump trick.

"Lead the Jack of clubs. The fact that you let him see the Jack makes it even more likely that he will be able to establish the suit with no more than a single loser. In fact, the Jack would be the right card from K-J-x as well. The full hand:

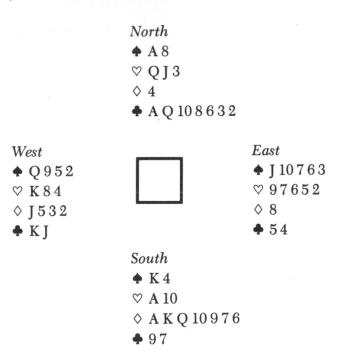

North
♠ A 8
♡ Q J 3
◇ 4
♣ A Q 10 8 6 3 2

West
♠ Q 9 5 2
♡ K 8 4
◇ J 5 3 2
♣ K J

East
♠ J 10 7 6 3
♡ 9 7 6 5 2
◇ 8
♣ 5 4

South
♠ K 4
♡ A 10
◇ A K Q 10 9 7 6
♣ 9 7

"Declarer knows he can establish the clubs by giving up the trick to the King, but why should he risk doing so, when there is the danger of a ruff? He goes up with the Ace and by the time he finds out he must lose a diamond trick, it is too late. On any other lead, he must make the contract.

"Not quite so clear is how to attack South's slam contract after the following bidding:

South	North
1♢	1♠
2♣	3♢
3NT	4♣
4NT	5♡
6♢	Pass

"Sitting West, you hold:

♠ K 7 6 2
♡ K 10 8 3
♢ 9 7 5
♣ 6 2

"It sounds as though the opponents have reached a 'momentum' slam, which may not be reached at the other table. So it is even more important for you to defeat it with your lead. How much do you know?

"North is surely short in hearts and declarer has few spades, so a trump lead seems promising. But wait! Neither opponent has indicated long trumps and both seem to have length in clubs. On such deals, it is rarely necessary to stop a crossruff, because declarer is unable to cash enough tricks in his long side suit—in this case, clubs. However, if he needs to pick up a 12th trick, you know that a spade finesse is going to succeed. How can you point him away from that line of play?

"What is partner going to contribute to the defense? From the fact that South didn't bid 5NT (as he did on the previous deal) it is possible that his side is missing an Ace—probably the Ace of hearts. If not, you can still hope for the Queen of hearts, because—yes, you are going to lead the King of hearts!

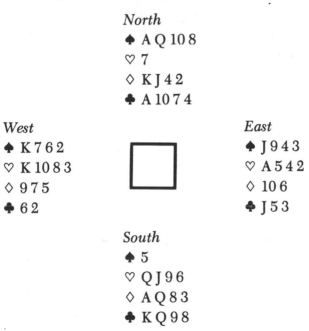

North
♠ A Q 10 8
♡ 7
◇ K J 4 2
♣ A 10 7 4

West
♠ K 7 6 2
♡ K 10 8 3
◇ 9 7 5
♣ 6 2

East
♠ J 9 4 3
♡ A 5 4 2
◇ 10 6
♣ J 5 3

South
♠ 5
♡ Q J 9 6
◇ A Q 8 3
♣ K Q 9 8

"When your King of hearts holds the first trick, you shift to a spade. Declarer may decide that your lead has made it unnecessary for him to rely on the spade finesse. All he needs is a ruffing finesse through your marked Ace of hearts, because he can ruff two spades and throw one on the established heart—except that when he runs the Queen of hearts, your partner takes the trick!

"Given any other lead, declarer simply must take the winning finesse in spades."

Benito gave one other deal, but it didn't add much to this sensational lead of the King of hearts, and as a matter of fact, there was a slight overstatement in the analysis. Did you notice, by the way, how the last deal tied up with Tony Priday's advice on the question of camouflage?

Having sharpened your mind by a study of Garozzo's thought-processes, see what you can make of a lead problem that arose in a match between Australia and Sweden in the 1977 Bermuda Bowl. At game all the bidding goes:

South	West	North	East
1NT	Pass	2♡	Pass
2♠	Pass	3♡	Pass
3♠	Pass	6#	Pass
Pass	Pass		

South's 1NT opening is 15-17, and North's response of two hearts is a transfer to spades. As West, what would you lead from:

♠ Q 8 7 4
♡ 10 8
◊ 10 7 5 4
♣ A Q 8

North is likely to hold five spades (at least), and South three spades. With four spades to the Queen and a side Ace, you must fancy a forcing game.

What do you make of the club situation? Players with singletons generally make some form of Ace-inquiry on the way to a slam. So North, in view of his leap to six spades, is probably void of clubs. To weaken the dummy while still holding the club Ace for a later force, West must *underlead* the Ace of clubs.

The exciting thing is that Anders Morath, of Sweden, who earlier in the year had won the Bols Brilliancy Prize at Elsinore, did so. The full hand was:

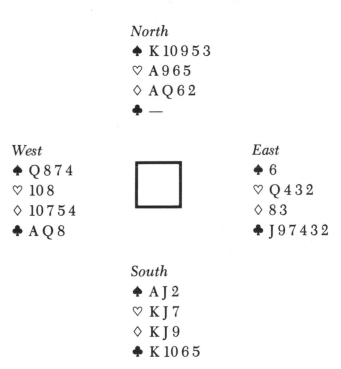

North
♠ K 10 9 5 3
♡ A 9 6 5
◇ A Q 6 2
♣ —

West
♠ Q 8 7 4
♡ 10 8
◇ 10 7 5 4
♣ A Q 8

East
♠ 6
♡ Q 4 3 2
◇ 8 3
♣ J 9 7 4 3 2

South
♠ A J 2
♡ K J 7
◇ K J 9
♣ K 10 6 5

Dick Cummings, the Australian declarer, in his own words, "accepted the force with the air of a man who does not enjoy early commitment." However, he found both major-suit Queens and laboriously slotted 12 tricks.

20. MICHEL LEBEL (FRANCE)

"Whenever dummy has a suit such as A-Q-10-9-x or K-Q-10-9-x, and appears to be short of entries, be willing to hold off with J-x."

Michel Lebel is one of many sharp, knowledgeable, young players in France who will keep their country in the forefront of international bridge when the giants of the last 20 years have hung up their boots.

Lebel first made his mark on the international bridge scene at the 1972 Olympiad in Miami, when France came fourth. He played also in Monte Carlo four years later, finishing in sixth place. In between, partnered by Paul Chemla, he won the first-ever European Pairs Championship and ventured into authorship, writing *La Majeure Cinquième* in collaboration with the old master, Pierre Jais.

Lebel's tip concerns an almost unexplored maneuver in the battlefield of communications:

"Successful defense often requires that you should take all possible measures to shut out dummy's long suit. Often, you will try to spoil the declarer's communications.

"Sitting over dummy's K-Q-10-9-x, you will, as a matter of course, hold off with A-J-x when dummy's King is played. But when the 10 is finessed? The position is essentially the same; to kill the suit it may be necessary to hold off, persuading the declarer to finesse the 9 next time. If you win the 10 with the Jack, he will have better communications, obviously.

"My tip is that you should sometimes hold up the Jack—*even when you do not possess the Ace.* You will find that quite remarkable results can be obtained. On the deal below, I held the East cards:

South dealer
Both sides vulnerable

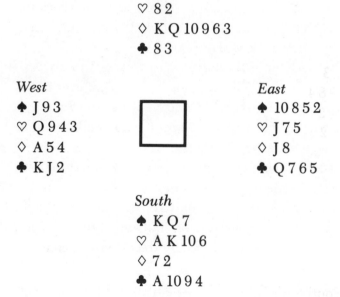

North
♠ A 6 4
♡ 8 2
◇ K Q 10 9 6 3
♣ 8 3

West
♠ J 9 3
♡ Q 9 4 3
◇ A 5 4
♣ K J 2

East
♠ 10 8 5 2
♡ J 7 5
◇ J 8
♣ Q 7 6 5

South
♠ K Q 7
♡ A K 10 6
◇ 7 2
♣ A 10 9 4

"South opened 1NT, North raised to 3NT, and West led the 3 of hearts, East's Jack losing to declarer's King.

South played a low diamond to dummy's 9 and East, without any hesitation, allowed the 9 to win!

"South quite naturally came back to his hand with a spade and repeated the finesse. When the 10 lost to the Jack, he could no longer make nine tricks as he was short of entries to bring in the diamonds.

"In the next example, after the same bidding, West led the Jack of spades against 3NT.

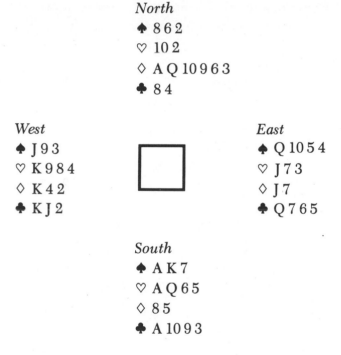

North
♠ 8 6 2
♡ 10 2
◊ A Q 10 9 6 3
♣ 8 4

West
♠ J 9 3
♡ K 9 8 4
◊ K 4 2
♣ K J 2

East
♠ Q 10 5 4
♡ J 7 3
◊ J 7
♣ Q 7 6 5

South
♠ A K 7
♡ A Q 6 5
◊ 8 5
♣ A 10 9 3

"South won the first trick with the King of spades, and ran the 8 of diamonds—which held the trick! South continued with the 5 of diamonds and paused when West produced a low diamond. Either West held K-J-x-x, thought South, in which case the contract was bound to fail, or East had tried a desperate measure, holding up the King from K-x.

"South decided to go up with the Ace, believing this was the only chance to win the contract—and he nearly fell off his chair when the Jack appeared. Once again, it is clear that holding up the Jack is the only way to lead the declarer astray.

"Extending the same principle, observe how the hold-up makes declarer's task more difficult on this deal:

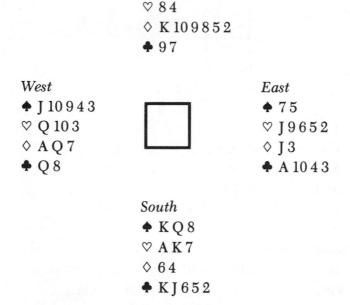

North
♠ A 6 2
♡ 8 4
◇ K 10 9 8 5 2
♣ 9 7

West
♠ J 10 9 4 3
♡ Q 10 3
◇ A Q 7
♣ Q 8

East
♠ 7 5
♡ J 9 6 5 2
◇ J 3
♣ A 10 4 3

South
♠ K Q 8
♡ A K 7
◇ 6 4
♣ K J 6 5 2

"West leads the Jack of spades against 3NT and South wins with the King. He leads the 4 of diamonds to the second trick, West plays the 7 and dummy the 8.

"If East wins with the Jack, the contract will surely be made, as South will easily establish the diamonds, with the Ace of spades for entry. But if East ducks the first diamond, South will come back to his hand with a heart and lead his second diamond. When West produces the Queen, the declarer may conclude that East has held up the Ace and that the suit is distributed in this fashion:

North
K 10 9 8 5 2

West   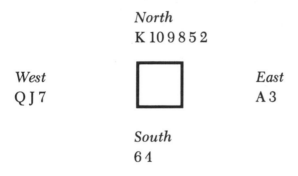   *East*
Q J 7   A 3

South
6 4

"If South forms this opinion, he will duck on the second round. It is true that East's hold-up, with A-x, would be a mistake, but it is not so unlikely a mistake.

"My bridge tip is this: whenever dummy has a suit such as A-Q-10-9-x or K-Q-10-9-x, and appears to be short of entries, be willing to hold off with J-x. You may well find that this daring maneuver offers the only real chance of preventing declarer from bringing in the long suit."

These hold-ups with J-x or A-J-x are certainly among the least known, or at any rate the least practiced, stratagems in the game. Let us begin by considering the example mentioned at the beginning of Lebel's tip, making the play more difficult by placing the long suit in the closed hand:

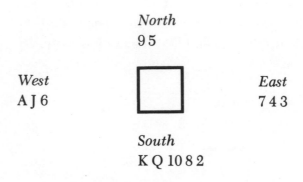

North
9 5

West
A J 6

East
7 4 3

South
K Q 10 8 2

The declarer, who is presumed to have one entry to hand, which cannot be driven out, runs the 9 from dummy. There is no likely division of the suit in which it can be wrong for West to hold up the Jack. Partner may hold Q-x-x, it is true, but then the hold-up will make no difference. After the 9 has held, declarer will, of course, finesse the 8 on the next round.

The defender would surely hold up if he held A-Q-x over the K-J-10, or A-K-x over the Q-J-10. In these situations, it is important to realize that the King, Queen, and Jack are all the same in trick-taking capacity. Here it is essential to hold up the Queen:

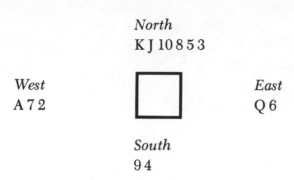

North
K J 10 8 5 3

West
A 7 2

East
Q 6

South
9 4

Assume, as before, that there is one entry to the hand that has the long suit. When South finesses the 9, East must hold off.

How would you expect the declarer to play the next combination?

North
K 10 9 8 4 2

West
A 7 5

East
J 6

South
Q 3

With one side entry to the table, South may lead the 3 and put in dummy's 8. If East takes the trick, declarer will overtake the Queen on the next round. The run of the suit can be prevented if East declines to part with the Jack and West holds up his Ace, for declarer will run the Queen on the second round, playing East for A-x.

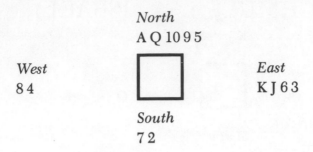

North
A Q 10 9 5

West
8 4

East
K J 6 3

South
7 2

South leads low and finesses the 10. Assume again, that there is one entry in the dummy, which cannot be forced out. If East captures the 10 with the Jack, South will develop three tricks in the suit; if East holds off, then declarer will finesse the 9 next time and end with just two tricks. The result in tricks would be the same in this example if East held J-x and West K-x-x-x.

Can it ever be right to hold up the 10, do you think? Consider this position:

North
K J 8 7 3

West
Q 6 2

East
A 10 4

South
9 5

South begins by running the 9—as good a way as any of playing the suit. If East wins, declarer will finesse again on the next round and will develop three tricks when dummy holds a side entry. But if East ducks, South will follow with a finesse of the 8 and may lack entries to develop any more tricks.

21. SCHMUEL LEV (ISRAEL)

"When you have a holding such as A-Q or A-J in the suit led by partner, do not automatically play 'Third hand high.'"

Israel did not join the European Bridge League until 1965, but growth since then has been rapid. In 1967, an official Hebrew bridge terminology was approved by the Academy of Language, and in 1975, Israel hosted the European Championships, finishing second to Italy, and so qualifying for the 1976 Bermuda Bowl in Monte Carlo. Israel came second to U.S.A. and Italy, and followed with a creditable performance in the Olympiad.

Many of the top Israeli players are of Polish origin, and Poland, of course, is one of the strongest bridge-playing nations in Europe. Schmuel Lev is one of the players most responsible for Israel's success. He is very much at home in big-money rubber bridge and has great stamina. In the Bermuda Bowl/Olympiad marathon, which lasted three weeks, he was putting in some of his best work at the end. His tip is of very wide application.

"One of the maxims that bridge inherited from whist was 'Third hand high.' Another slogan that expressed the same idea was 'Never finesse against your partner.'

"Since the early days, of course, a great deal has

been discovered. My tip describes some quite frequent situations where it may be good play for third hand to finesse against his partner—that is, to play the lower of non-touching honors—even when dummy has a worthless holding in the suit led.

"A common situation occurs in notrumps. It is often vital to winkle out declarer's stopper on the first round, so that the suit can be run when defenders next obtain the lead:

North
♠ J 10 9
♡ A K 9 2
♢ K Q 10 5
♣ 5 3

West
♠ 5
♡ 4 3
♢ 9 8 7 4 2
♣ Q 9 8 4 2

East
♠ K Q 8 6 2
♡ Q 8 7 6
♢ 3
♣ A J 7

South
♠ A 7 4 3
♡ J 10 5
♢ A J 6
♣ K 10 6

"West leads the 4 of clubs against South's contract of 3 NT. If East puts up the Ace (third hand high!), South will duck the next round of clubs and West's suit will be dead. South will be able to develop his ninth trick by taking a heart finesse into the safe hand.

"But if East plays the Jack of clubs on the first round, it will be too dangerous for South to duck. He would look very foolish if West's clubs were A-Q-9-x-x and a single heart finesse would have won the contract.

"Of course, there is sometimes an element of risk when you finesse against your partner. Here, East will be giving declarer an unnecessary trick if his clubs are Q-x-x. But East can afford to take this risk, for he has control of the major suits and can see that the contract will be defeated if West's club suit can be brought in. East also knows that West cannot possibly have a side entry, so it is essential to establish a lifeline between the defending hands.

"Against a suit contract, a finesse at trick one may create an entry for a vital switch later in the play:

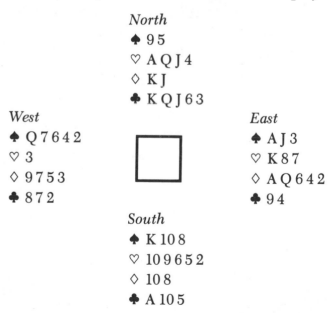

North
♠ 9 5
♡ A Q J 4
◇ K J
♣ K Q J 6 3

West
♠ Q 7 6 4 2
♡ 3
◇ 9 7 5 3
♣ 8 7 2

East
♠ A J 3
♡ K 8 7
◇ A Q 6 4 2
♣ 9 4

South
♠ K 10 8
♡ 10 9 6 5 2
◇ 10 8
♣ A 10 5

"North-South are playing Precision and the bidding goes:

South	West	North	East
—	—	1♣	Pass
1♡	Pass	1NT	Pass
2◇	Pass	4♡	Pass
Pass	Pass		

"In this sequence, the opening one club in conventional, South's one heart is natural and positive, and North's 1NT asks for controls. South's two diamonds indicated three Neapolitan controls (2 for an Ace, 1 for a King). Realizing that no slam is possible, North bids a direct game.

"West leads the 4 of spades and East, in view of the bidding, can gauge the hand very accurately. He knows that South must hold an Ace and a King, so there can be no advantage in going up with the Ace of spades. On the contrary, East must insert the Jack, to drive out South's King. When East comes in with the King of hearts, he leads a low spade to his partner's Queen. The obvious diamond switch then defeats the contract.

"A defender who has bid a suit may often have an opportunity to finesse against partner when this suit is led:

North
- ♠ Q J 7 2
- ♡ 10 9 4
- ◇ K Q J 10
- ♣ A Q

West
- ♠ 5
- ♡ J 5 3 2
- ◇ 9 3 2
- ♣ 8 7 6 5 4

East
- ♠ A 4
- ♡ A Q 8 6
- ◇ A 8 4
- ♣ K 9 3 2

South
- ♠ K 10 9 8 6 3
- ♡ K 7
- ◇ 7 6 5
- ♣ J 10

"South becomes declarer in four spades after East has opened one heart. West leads the 2 of hearts, which suggests he has an honor in the suit. East therefore finesses the Queen, forcing the King. When East comes in with the Ace of spades, it is quite safe for him to underlead the Ace of hearts, because West is likely to hold the Jack; in any case, there is no other hope of defeating the contract. When West obtains the lead with the Jack of hearts, he naturally switches to a club, establishing a trick in this suit before the Ace of diamonds has been forced out.

"My bridge tip is this: when you have a holding such as A-Q or A-J in the suit led by partner, do not automatically play third hand high. By finessing the lower honor, you may be able to create a vital entry to your partner's hand."

There are, indeed, many exceptions to the old rule of "third hand high" and, still more, "second hand low." Some occasions where the third player should finesse against partner for reasons of communication were described in connection with Rixi Markus's tip.

It is generally right for third hand to insert the middle card in this type of situation:

North
5

West   *East*
K 9 7 4 2   A J 6

South
Q 10 8 3

It is unlikely, after the lead of the 4, that the defense can run five tricks, and communications are better maintained if East plays the Jack on the first round.

Players seldom make the right play in this position:

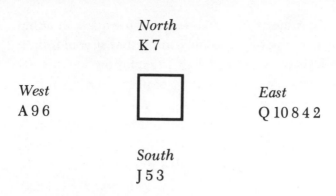

North

K 7

West

A 9 6

East

Q 10 8 4 2

South

J 5 3

Assume that East has a poor hand with no quick entry. When West leads the 6 and dummy plays low, it is plain that the lead, against notrumps, is from A-x-x or J-x-x. If from A-x-x, it is essential for East to play the 10, not the Queen. (Note that the lead of the Ace, in line with Jeremy Flint's tip, would simplify the position.)

In suit contracts, provided you are reasonably certain that partner has not underled an Ace, it is important to play the Jack from K-J-x or any longer suit headed by K-J. There are three reasons for this:

1. It is a discovery play: you find out whether declarer has A-Q or just the Ace—in other words, whether there are tricks to be made in the suit later.

2. If the jack forces the Ace, partner will be willing later to lead from the Queen; but if the King is headed by the Ace, it may be much more risky for partner to underlead the Queen next time, on occasions when this would suit the defense.

3. To some extent, you deceived the declarer about the lie of the cards. You may think that it could make no difference whether East, defending against six spades on the deal below, were to play the King or Jack of clubs on the opening lead—but watch!

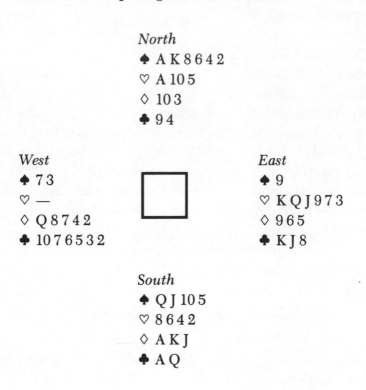

North
♠ A K 8 6 4 2
♡ A 10 5
◊ 10 3
♣ 9 4

West
♠ 7 3
♡ —
◊ Q 8 7 4 2
♣ 10 7 6 5 3 2

East
♠ 9
♡ K Q J 9 7 3
◊ 9 6 5
♣ K J 8

South
♠ Q J 10 5
♡ 8 6 4 2
◊ A K J
♣ A Q

East opened a weak two hearts, South doubled, and North bid three hearts. Thus, South became the declarer in six spades and West, following the modern style of second-best from weak suits, led the 7 of clubs. East played the King and South won. Deciding that

East had already shown his ration for a weak two bid, South drew trumps and played off A-K-J of diamonds, discarding a heart from dummy and leaving West on play.

If East had played the Jack of clubs at trick one, the position would not have been so clear. South might place West with the King of clubs, and East with the Queen of diamonds. If he took that view and finessed the Jack of diamonds, he would lose the contract. The King and Jack of clubs appear to be equals, but some equals are not so equal as others.

22. BILLY EISENBERG (U.S.A.)

"Play low from dummy when it can't cost you a trick and may cause third hand to make a grievous error."

Billy Eisenberg first became a national figure in the game when, at the age of 30, he was asked to join the original Dallas Aces. He stayed with the Aces for three years, winning the world championship in 1970 and 1971. He has since won twice more. Each of the four victories was gained with a different partner.

All players have some sort of tag attached to them. "Machine-like" is the word often applied to Billy, and it describes well the accuracy of his game. It does not quite fit his personality. At the table and away from it, Billy is thoroughly relaxed—he exudes the easy and confident life-style of California where he now lives.

Billy's bridge tip explains how to put pressure on the defender in third position. Especially at trick one, this player may be uncertain whether to finesse against the dummy or make sure of winning the trick.

"Most declarers realize the advantage of playing low from dummy when the Queen is led through a King. The Ace is almost certainly residing over the King, and by playing low once or twice from dummy, you may bring down the Ace on your right, establishing the King as a trick.

"However, there are many other holdings where

declarer can gain a full trick by playing low from dummy in situations that are not so well known.

"For my first example, I would like to show you a hand that I played in the Houston Playoffs determining the U.S. team for the 1977 world championship:

North dealer
Both sides vulnerable

North
♠ K J 8 5
♡ Q 4
◊ K J 4 2
♣ A Q 7

West
♠ 10 9 6 4 2
♡ J 7
◊ 10 6 5 3
♣ 10 2

East
♠ A 7 3
♡ K 9 2
◊ A Q 9 8 7
♣ 8 4

South
♠ Q
♡ A 10 8 6 5 3
◊ —
♣ K J 9 6 5 3

South	West	North	East
—	—	1NT	Pass
2 ◇ (1)	Pass	2 ♡	Pass
3 ♣ (2)	Pass	3NT	Pass
4 ♣ (3)	Pass	5 ♣	Pass
6 ♣ (4)	Pass	Pass	Pass

(1) Jacoby transfer; (2) Game force; (3) Slam try; (4) We were behind at the time.

Opening lead: 5 of diamonds (3rd or 5th best).

"When West led a low diamond, I immediately played low from dummy. Why? Why not play the Jack, hoping that West had underled the Queen?

"Well, if West really had led away from the Queen, East was going to have to make a pretty good play of the 10 from A-10 if he happened to hold that card. Most players would play the Ace. Besides, there was a strong possibility that East held both Ace and Queen, in which case, playing the Jack from dummy would be no use at all.

"All in all, I felt the percentages were strongly in my favor to play low from dummy as the best way to build up a diamond trick for a spade discard.

"As it happened, East, fearing his partner might have led from 5-3 doubleton, played the Queen. I ruffed, entered dummy with a club, and led the King of diamonds, establishing a discard for my losing spade. All I lost was a heart. Had I played the Jack from dummy at trick one, I would have lost the slam.

"There are many occasions when you can put tons of pressure on your right-hand opponent by playing a low card from dummy."

North dealer
Neither side vulnerable

North
♠ K 7 5
♡ A 7 4
◇ Q J 6
♣ A 8 7 4

West
♠ J 6 4
♡ Q 9 3 2
◇ K 10 8 4
♣ J 9

East
♠ 3
♡ J 10 6
◇ A 9 7 3 2
♣ Q 10 3 2

South
♠ A Q 10 9 8 2
♡ K 8 5
◇ 5
♣ K 6 5

South	West	North	East
—	—	1♣	Pass
1♠	Pass	1NT	Pass
4♠	Pass	Pass	Pass

Opening lead: 4 of diamonds.

"Breathes there a declarer among us who would not put up a diamond honor from dummy at trick one? The result of this play is that if East wins and does not return the suit (allowing South to discard a loser and discard again on the established diamond honor), South will lose a trick in each suit outside the trump suit and make only four-odd.

"Now, let's see what happens if South plays low from dummy at trick one. It is going to take a pretty brave East player to insert the 9 and run the risk of losing to a singleton 10 in the declarer's hand, or possibly a doubleton 10 if West's lead was from K-8-4 originally.

"Most East players will surely play the Ace. This will enable South to make a routine loser-on-loser play in diamonds for the precious overtrick.

"The play also picks up a trick when East started with both Ace and King, but not the 10. Surely nobody (unless he had studied this Bols Tip) would insert an 8 or 9 from A-K-8-x or A-K-9-x when dummy played low. Right?

"Here is one more example where declarer picked

up an overtrick for a top score by making an unorthodox play from dummy at trick one:

West dealer
Both sides vulnerable

North
♠ A 8 4
♡ A 10 9
◇ A J 3
♣ K 9 7 6

West
♠ K 10
♡ K J 2
◇ Q 10 6 2
♣ Q J 8 4

East
♠ 3
♡ Q 7 6 5 4
◇ K 9 8 5 4
♣ 10 2

South
♠ Q J 9 7 6 5 2
♡ 8 3
◇ 7
♣ A 5 3

South	West	North	East
—	1♣	1NT	Pass
4♠	Pass	Pass	Pass

Opening lead: 2 of diamonds.

"South played low from dummy, knowing full well that even if East won the trick cheaply, the Ace would always furnish a quick discard.

"What was East to do? Play the 8? Would you? If partner had led from Q-x-x and declarer had 10-x, the trick might not come back. In any event, East was not up to the play of the 8. He went up with the King and shifted to a heart. South discarded a heart on the Ace of diamonds, came to hand with a club, picked up the King of spades and ran off all the trumps, squeezing West in diamonds and clubs. The Jack of diamonds became a threat-card only because of the play at trick one.

"My bridge tip is this: to drive the opponents crazy and gain extra tricks by the cartload, play low from dummy when it can't cost you a trick and may cause third hand to make a grievous error."

The reader may have noted that South had an alternative play on the last deal. Instead of playing to squeeze West, he can discard a club on the Ace of diamonds and attempt to establish a 13th club by ruffing the third round. As the cards lie, this doesn't work so well.

Eisenberg gave one other deal, showing the North and East hands only:

North dealer
Both sides vulnerable

North
♠ K 7 6
♡ J 10 5 3
◇ A K J 8 4
♣ 10

```
┌─────────┐
│         │
│         │
│         │
└─────────┘
```

East
♠ A J 5 4 3
♡ 9
◇ 7 6 5
♣ J 8 5 3

South	West	North	East
—	—	1◇	Pass
1♡	Pass	2♡	Pass
4♡	Pass	Pass	Pass

Opening lead: 2 of spades.

When declarer plays low from dummy, East has a difficult decision. His partner may have led from the Queen, in which case, the play of the Ace would give away a trick. On the other hand, to finesse the Jack could be wrong in a number of situations. The point is that declarer, holding either a singleton or doubleton spade, should not, as a rule, go up with the King in the faint hope that West has underled the Ace.

Most of the Bols entries from America dealt with rather general subjects. This was the only one to give advice about a clearly defined area of play—and very good advice, too.

There was a well-known deal in one of the Bermuda Bowl encounters between Italy and the U.S.A., when the club suit was divided as follows:

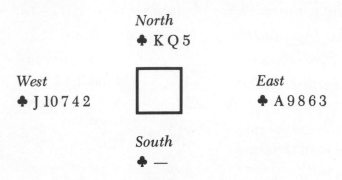

North
♣ K Q 5

West
♣ J 10 7 4 2

East
♣ A 9 8 6 3

South
♣ —

At one table, West led a low club, not the Jack, against a slam contract. The Italian declarer played the Queen from dummy and finished a trick short. If he had played a low club instead, it would have been difficult for East to finesse the 8, and if East had made the wrong decision, South would have had good chances to make the slam.

Note, too, that with K-Q-x in dummy, and a singleton in hand, it is right to play low when the suit is led. There is always a chance (if West has led low from the Jack) that East will contribute the Ace.

23. PEDRO-PAULO ASSUMPÇÃO (BRAZIL)

"When more than one play is needed to make the contract, give special thought to the best sequence. The order may be no less important than the plays themselves."

Urbane and courteous are words that describe "P.P.," as he is known throughout the world of bridge. These are qualities which have played a part in Brazil's climb to Great Power status in the world of bridge, crowned with the 1976 Olympiad win over Italy. They take their bridge seriously down South America way, and Latin temperament can have a low flash point. Chagas, the brilliant and restless schemer, has been well served by his constant partner.

P.P.'s tip is entitled, "The Secret is in the Timing."

"In most deals, the declarer soon identifies the plays he must make for the contract, such as establishing a suit, knocking out an entry, and so forth.

"But however good his reasoning, success may still elude him, unless he makes these plays in precisely the right order. In bridge, the secret is often in the timing.

"Whenever there is more than one step to be taken, you should take special care to select the best timing. Ask yourself whether the obvious sequence of play will, in fact, produce the required result. Whenever there is doubt, try the effect of a change in the timing.

West dealer
East-West vulnerable

```
                    North
                    ♠ A 7 4
                    ♡ 7 5 4
                    ◇ K 6
                    ♣ A J 10 6 5

West                                    East
♠ Q 3               ┌─────────┐         ♠ J 10 9 5 2
♡ Q J 10 8 6        │         │         ♡ 9 3 2
◇ A J 4             │         │         ◇ 10 7 2
♣ K 7 3             └─────────┘         ♣ Q 4

                    South
                    ♠ K 8 6
                    ♡ A K
                    ◇ Q 9 8 5 3
                    ♣ 9 8 2
```

South	West	North	East
—	1♡	Pass	Pass
1NT	Pass	3NT	Pass
Pass	Pass		

"You are in 3NT and West leads the Queen of hearts. It is easy to see where the tricks must come from. You have only four tricks in the major suits, so must plan to take four club tricks and a trick in diamonds.

"Many players, however, would get the timing of this hand quite wrong. Would you?

"Suppose you play clubs first, as may perhaps seem natural. In that case, your last heart stopper is driven out and you never have time to make a diamond trick.

"So, play a diamond at trick two! If West plays the Ace, you make four diamond tricks—enough for the contract—and if West ducks, you come to hand with a spade and attack clubs. The timing, you see, makes all the difference.

"On the next deal, three distinct steps are needed and there is only one correct sequence.

West dealer
North-South vulnerable

<table>
<tr><td></td><td>North</td><td></td></tr>
<tr><td></td><td>♠ 10 6 5</td><td></td></tr>
<tr><td></td><td>♡ K 6 4</td><td></td></tr>
<tr><td></td><td>◊ 8 4 2</td><td></td></tr>
<tr><td></td><td>♣ K 9 8 2</td><td></td></tr>
</table>

West		*East*
♠ Q 9 4		♠ J 7
♡ J 10 8		♡ A 9 7 3 2
◊ Q J 5 3		◊ 10 6
♣ Q 10 4		♣ J 6 5 3

<table>
<tr><td>South</td></tr>
<tr><td>♠ A K 8 3 2</td></tr>
<tr><td>♡ Q 5</td></tr>
<tr><td>◊ A K 9 7</td></tr>
<tr><td>♣ A 7</td></tr>
</table>

South	West	North	East
1♠	Pass	1NT	Pass
3◇	Pass	3♠	Pass
4♠	Pass	Pass	Pass

"West leads the Jack of hearts and you win with the Queen. You hope for a 3-2 trump break, but you may still need to look after the fourth diamond. You want to be able to ruff the last diamond, if necessary, but meanwhile you mustn't allow the opponents to play three rounds of trumps, and you must take care not to be overruffed by the hand that has only a doubleton spade. The question is, what is the best timing?

"It would be a mistake to draw two rounds of trumps early on, and also a mistake to begin with three rounds of diamond, allowing East to overruff dummy on the fourth round. The right sequence is to duck a diamond at trick two! When you regain the lead you cash A-K of trumps and go on your way rejoicing.

"Good timing is especially necessary when there is a danger of being shortened in trumps.

"West leads the Jack of hearts, East wins with the King and follows with the Ace. You ruff and note, that to make this optimistic contract, you will need to draw trumps, establish the clubs, and build up a 10th trick with the King of diamonds. You may be hopeful about the diamond King after East has shown up with the top hearts, but you still have to find the best sequence.

North dealer
North-South vulnerable

                    North
                    ♠ A K 6
                    ♡ 8 7 5 3
                    ◊ K 8 6
                    ♣ K 6 2

West   *East*
♠ 10 8 3   ♠ 9 2
♡ J 10 9 4   ♡ A K 6 2
◊ A J 4   ◊ Q 10 7 5 3
♣ Q J 4   ♣ 10 3

                    South
                    ♠ Q J 7 5 4
                    ♡ Q
                    ◊ 9 2
                    ♣ A 9 8 7 5

South	*West*	*North*	*East*
—	—	1♣	Pass
1♠	Pass	1NT	Pass
3♣	Pass	3♠	Pass
4♠	Pass	Pass	Pass

"Suppose you draw trumps and give up a club. A heart comes back and you ruff with your last trump. This way, you will never make a trick with the king of diamonds, because West will keep, for his last two cards, the Ace of diamonds and a heart.

"The only correct play is to lead a diamond early on. West can do no better than win and return a heart. You ruff and play a low club from each hand. Now, if another heart comes back, you can afford to ruff for the third time, as you can draw trumps from dummy and cash the clubs.

"My bridge tip is this: when more than one play is needed to make the contract, give special thought to the best sequence. You may well find that the order in which you make your plays is no less important than the plays themselves."

Assumpção used three deals of a familiar type to illustrate a novel approach to planning: identify the plays you need to make, then determine the best order.

At notrumps, to attack first the entries of the danger hand is a common stratagem; in a suit contract, the play tends to be less obvious.

South plays in four spades after East has opened 1NT. The defense begins with a diamond to the Ace, followed by ◊ Q. In a heat of the Philip Morris pairs, most of the South players rushed straight to their doom. They led a trump to the Queen and Ace, ruffed the third diamond, and ran out of steam when they found the trumps 4-1. There was no time now to enjoy the fourth round of clubs.

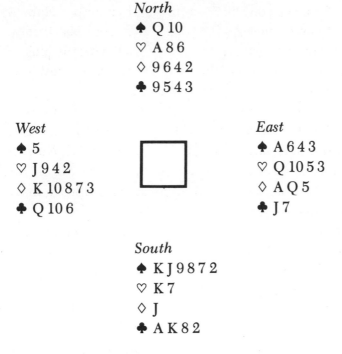

North
♠ Q 10
♡ A 8 6
◇ 9 6 4 2
♣ 9 5 4 3

West
♠ 5
♡ J 9 4 2
◇ K 10 8 7 3
♣ Q 10 6

East
♠ A 6 4 3
♡ Q 10 5 3
◇ A Q 5
♣ J 7

South
♠ K J 9 8 7 2
♡ K 7
◇ J
♣ A K 8 2

At only one table did the declarer appreciate that West was likely to hold the long diamonds and was therefore the danger hand. His possible entry must be driven out first. The best sequence, after the second diamond had been ruffed, is the club Aces, heart to Ace, club to King, third round of clubs. West forces again, but when East comes in with the Ace of spades, he has no diamond to lead.

The defenders can time plays carefully also. Here is an example of defensive timing by Chagas and Assumpção themselves, when they won the 1979 Sunday Times Pairs:

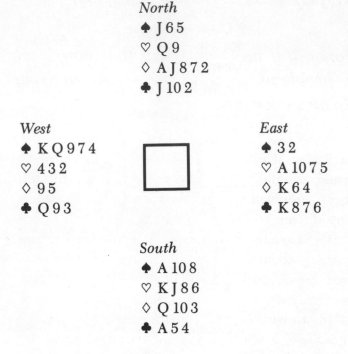

North
♠ J 6 5
♡ Q 9
◇ A J 8 7 2
♣ J 10 2

West
♠ K Q 9 7 4
♡ 4 3 2
◇ 9 5
♣ Q 9 3

East
♠ 3 2
♡ A 10 7 5
◇ K 6 4
♣ K 8 7 6

South
♠ A 10 8
♡ K J 8 6
◇ Q 10 3
♣ A 5 4

Defenders against 3NT, P.P. decided to retain his spade honors over the declarer and led ♣ 3. Dummy played the Jack and East ducked. The Queen of hearts was led from dummy, won by the Ace. Chagas, realizing that a trick in spades would be needed to beat the contract, now suspended the declarer on a hook by returning, not a club, but ♠ 3. When South ducked, P.P. reverted to ♣ Q, establishing five tricks for the defense.

24. JEFF RUBENS (U.S.A.)

"Honor thy partner. Show that you treat his problems as your own and actively help him solve them."

In a *Bridge World* of 1961, I recently came across a learned article, *The Doctor's Diagnosis*, by Jeff Rubens, to which was attached a note by the editor, Sonny Moyse:

"We have a feeling that readers would like to know something about our contributors—particularly new names. So we asked Rubens for a dossier and he answers thusly:

"'In answer to your query, yes, I am an undergraduate, a senior in the College of Arts and Sciences. I study mathematics, plan to go on to graduate school next year. I am 19 years old. Bridgewise, I am President of the Cornell Bridge Club and Chairman of the Tournament Committee.'"

"Nineteen! (Sigh.) It will, we're sure, please readers—as it has pleased us—to get this further evidence of the robust new blood in bridge. Heaven knows the United States can use it! Thus, we welcome Rubens, not only to our roster of top-notch contributors, but to high-level bridge."

The precocious talent was fully maintained. Rubens won the Spingold in 1972, and represented North America in the 1973 Bermuda Bowl. He is the author of such profound works as *Secrets of Winning Bridge* (published in Britain by Robert Hale) and co-editor with Edgar Kaplan of the *Bridge World;* all this is in addition to a successful career as an academic. Jeff has a lawyer's type of face, clever and narrow, with pronounced dark eyebrows.

That partners, by and large, are obtuse and likely to do the wrong thing, is a proposition to which we would all agree. Jeff Rubens offers counsel on this matter in a tip entitled "Honor Thy Partner."

"Car A signals for a left turn, but starts to turn right, then suddenly brakes to a stop. Whereupon Car B, traveling behind car A at a normal distance and speed, crashes into a tree.

"Bridge crashes are often of this sort. One of the defenders makes a losing play, but his partner was at fault. There is not only a loss on the deal, but also a drop in partnership morale. We seem to mind more when partner causes us to make the fatal move than when he makes it himself.

"A player should be alert to partner's problems as well as his own. Everyone tries to help partner by signalling, but better players should aim to go much further.

"For example, a good partner tries to remove undesirable options. If you can see that it would be a losing play for partner to duck with an Ace in front of dummy's K-J, prevent it by leading the suit yourself. If you cannot get in to lead the suit, perhaps you can discard the Queen behind dummy's K-J!

"Everyone knows those end positions when, by cashing a winner near the finish, you put partner to a guess. Always consider whether it might be better to lead a suit to which you know partner will follow.

"Where players fall down is in failing to notice that partner may have a problem. Once the problem is seen, protective measures are usually quite simple.

South dealer
East-West vulnerable

```
                        North
                        ♠ K 10 9 8
                        ♡ Q 9
                        ◇ A 10 9 4
                        ♣ Q 10 3

West                    ┌─────┐              East
♠ 5 4                   │     │              ♠ A Q 7 3
♡ K 10 8 7 5            │     │              ♡ A 6
◇ 8 6                   └─────┘              ◇ K 7 5 2
♣ 9 7 4 2                                    ♣ 8 6 5

                        South
                        ♠ J 6 2
                        ♡ J 4 3 2
                        ◇ Q J 3
                        ♣ A K J
```

South	West	North	East
1♣	Pass	1♠	Pass
1NT	Pass	3NT	Pass
Pass	Pass		

"West leads the 7 of hearts against 3NT and you win with the Ace. The heart position is easy to read: if the 7 is fourth best, West must hold the King, since he would have led the Jack from J-10-8-7. The defense should therefore be able to take two spades, two hearts, and a diamond. But there is a danger: if you return a heart at trick two, partner will duck, playing you for A-x-x. Then the King of hearts will be lost to the defense. To avoid this, lead something else at trick two, such as the 8 of clubs. Leave the heart return till later—best of all, until you have already notched four defensive tricks.

"You can keep even a sleepy partner from harm by removing his losing choice altogether.

South dealer
Both sides vulnerable

North
♠ 9 6
♡ K J 5
◇ Q J 10 8 6
♣ 10 8 6

West
♠ K 10 7 5 4
♡ Q 6 4 3
◇ A 2
♣ K 9

East
♠ A 8 3 2
♡ 9 7 2
◇ 4 3
♣ J 7 5 3

South
♠ Q J
♡ A 10 8
◇ K 9 7 5
♣ A Q 4 2

"South opens 1NT and all pass. Sitting West, you lead the 5 of spades to the 6, Ace, and Jack. East returns the 2 of spades, and you win with the King.

"You can see seven tricks—seven so long as a club is established before the Ace of diamonds has been forced out. But if you return the 4 of spades, partner may win and return a spade. You will win the argument that follows, but South will make the contract.

"Avoid this by returning, not the 4 of spades, but the 7. Partner will hardly overtake this to lead another spade, and when he wins the fourth round, the club shift will be more or less forced.

South dealer
North-South vulnerable

```
                      North
                      ♠ K J 7
                      ♡ A Q 8
                      ◇ A Q 8
                      ♣ K Q 7 4

West                  ┌─────┐              East
♠ 10 9 8              │     │              ♠ 6 5 3 2
♡ J 9 7 5             │     │              ♡ 10 4 2
◇ J 9 7 5             └─────┘              ◇ 10 4
♣ 9 8                                      ♣ J 10 6 5

                      South
                      ♠ A Q 4
                      ♡ K 6 3
                      ◇ K 6 3 2
                      ♣ A 3 2
```

"South opens 1NT and North, beating around no bushes, raises straight to 7NT. West leads the 10 of spades.

"Playing shrewdly, South cashes three spades, King and Ace of clubs, then leads a club to dummy's Queen. Poor West now has a ghastly decision, with over 2,000 points hanging on whether he parts with a diamond or a heart.

"Since neither suit has been played, can East help his partner in any way? Think about it.

"When South fails to lay down his cards at trick one, the whole deal is an open book to East. South must hold both red Kings, so he has 12 tricks on top. The defense will have a problem only if West holds four cards of each red suit and will be in trouble when he has to find a discard.

"If East addresses his mind to this problem in time, he can help his partner by vigorous suit-preference play, first with the 6 of spades, then with the Jack of clubs. This says to West, 'Don't bother about hearts, but if you have four diamonds, cling to them!'

"My bridge tip is this: Honor thy partner. Show that you treat his problems as your own and actively help him solve them. Amazingly, this will improve not only partner's defense, but also his overall performance. He will be playing more carefully in order to be worthy of your respect."

Entries for the Bols competition tended to become longer and more explicit as time went by, and I have somewhat shortened Rubens's contribution without, I trust, losing any of the points he made.

Much damage is caused to partnership cooperation by the ingrained habit of playing high in third position on the opening lead. In these examples, West has led "top of nothing":

North
K J 9

West	East
6 led	10 7 4 2

West leads the 6 and dummy plays the 9. It is silly, either in a suit contract or notrumps, to cover with the 10. Declarer will win with the Ace and West may uselessly pursue the same attack when next in the lead. From his point of view, you might hold Q-10-x.

It is doubly foolish to contribute a high honor that cannot possibly promote a trick:

North
Q 10 6

West	East
5 led	K 8 7 3

Declarer, holding A-J-9 or A-J-9-x, will put in the Queen, partly to smoke out the King, partly to conceal his strength. If East, with K-x-x or K-x-x-x, covers the Queen, then declarer will have achieved both his objectives and West will be left in the dark. Again:

North

K 7 4

West		*East*
6 led		J 9 5 2

Here it looks as though partner has led into declarer's A-Q-10-8. Don't make the damage worse by playing the Jack, for then declarer will win with the Ace, and West may cherish the belief that he has made a sagacious opening toward his partner's Q-J-9-x-x.

Pursuing the theme that a defender should strive to remove his partner's losing options, Rubens later proposed a name for all those plays which have as their special object the provision of help for partner—"The Bols Coup." (The play proposed by Peter Swinnerton-Dyer in the deal described on page 160 is an excellent example.) Sometimes it helps to cash a winner in an outside suit before leading the critical suit. Rubens gave this example:

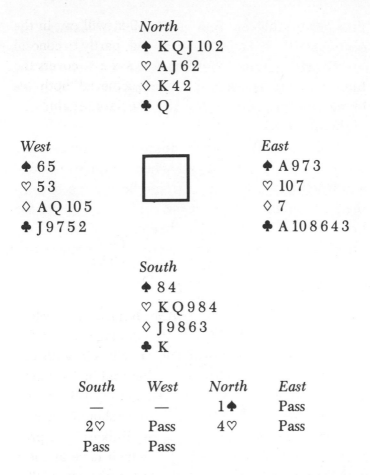

North
- ♠ K Q J 10 2
- ♡ A J 6 2
- ◇ K 4 2
- ♣ Q

West
- ♠ 6 5
- ♡ 5 3
- ◇ A Q 10 5
- ♣ J 9 7 5 2

East
- ♠ A 9 7 3
- ♡ 10 7
- ◇ 7
- ♣ A 10 8 6 4 3

South
- ♠ 8 4
- ♡ K Q 9 8 4
- ◇ J 9 8 6 3
- ♣ K

South	West	North	East
—	—	1♠	Pass
2♡	Pass	4♡	Pass
Pass	Pass		

"West led a club to East's Ace, and East made the obvious shift to the 7 of diamonds. South covered with the 8, and West (looking to East to hold the spade Ace or heart King, and at least one more diamond) made the obvious play of the 10. South then made a few obvious plays of his own and wound up discarding three diamonds on dummy's spades, making his contract.

"Obvious or not, West's defense was reasonable. East's was not. He should have removed his partner's losing choice *by cashing the Ace of spades* before leading his diamond!"

And there is the opposite situation: a defender may try to give his partner a ruff when no ruff is possible and when some other move would have succeeded. In these situations, too, a player can often remove the losing option. But the signals that tell partner *not* to try for a ruff are, says Rubens, more difficult to convey:

North dealer
Neither side vulnerable

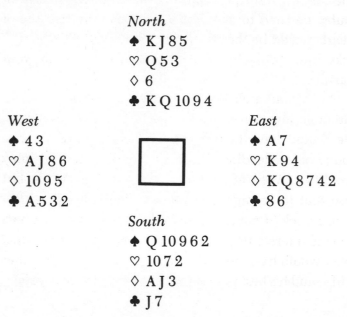

North
♠ K J 8 5
♡ Q 5 3
◇ 6
♣ K Q 10 9 4

West
♠ 4 3
♡ A J 8 6
◇ 10 9 5
♣ A 5 3 2

East
♠ A 7
♡ K 9 4
◇ K Q 8 7 4 2
♣ 8 6

South
♠ Q 10 9 6 2
♡ 10 7 2
◇ A J 3
♣ J 7

South	West	North	East
—	—	1♣	1♦
1♠	2♦	2♠	Pass
Pass	3♦	Pass	Pass
3♠	Pass	Pass	Pass

"East and West were both good players and were testing out a partnership. West led the 10 of diamonds; which was followed by the 6, Queen, Ace. South led the 10 of spades to East's Ace; and East, appreciating that it might be necessary to put West in to attack hearts, shifted to the 8 of clubs."

A shift now to the heart Jack would have produced the desired result, but after West put on the Ace of clubs, he tried to give East a ruff, hoping the Ace of hearts would be the re-entry for a second ruff. "Well," asks Rubens, "which one would you want as your partner?"

"East had a clear chance to solve West's problem, although few players would think of the correct play. He should have held up the Ace of trumps for one round before leading clubs! It is not only that this play would put West off the idea of getting two ruffs, but also that in ambiguous situations, holding off with a trump trick (if not required for other purposes) suggests lack of interest in getting a ruff. Had East done this, West would have been warned against trying for a club ruff—and his best play is to shift to the Jack of hearts!"

THE AWARDS FOR
BRIDGE TIPS 16 TO 24

The nine entries for the third year of the competition were judged by a panel of no fewer than 40 experts. To remind you, the entries were:

1. DOROTHY HAYDEN TRUSCOTT: *Indicate attitude to the opening leader's suit with the first spot card.*

2. PER-OLOV SUNDELIN: *If you won't beat the contract by winning the trick, duck it.*

3. TONY PRIDAY: *If you can mislead the declarer in one suit, he may form a wrong conclusion about another.*

4. BENITO GAROZZO: *Against a slam contract, attack with the opening lead.*

5. MICHEL LEBEL: *When dummy is short of entries, be prepared to hold up with J-x.*

6. SCHMUEL LEV: *Do not automatically play "third hand high" from a holding such as A-Q or A-J.*

7. BILLY EISENBERG: *Play low from dummy when this may put pressure on third hand.*

8. PEDRO-PAULO ASSUMPÇÃO: *Having decided*

what plays are necessary, give thought to the best sequence.

9. JEFF RUBENS: *Work out your partner's problems and help him to solve them.*

How would you have voted this time?

The opinions of the 40 judges varied widely, as may be imagined. Almost the only consistent feature was that all gave a good mark to Rubens's advice to consider partner's problems. The total marks were very even, the averages ranging from 13 to 16½ out of 20. The scores for the first three were:

1. *Jeff Rubens* (honor thy partner), 662 points.

2. *Dorothy Hayden Truscott* (show attitude to the suit led), 618 points.

3. *Tony Priday* (misrepresent one suit to mislead in another), 614 points.

As in previous years, one could see that the panel judged by different standards. If the object was to suggest a new train of thought to experienced tournament players, then Tony Priday's piece on anti-discovery was the most profound, but columnists with a wide readership may have thought his advice was pitched at too high a level. As an immediate points-winner, I liked especially Sundelin's recommendation not to release a guard in the opponent's side suit, and Eisenberg's advice to put third hand on the spot by playing low from dummy in certain circumstances. The particular merit of the winning entry was that the concept of nursing partner is one that scarcely enters the mind of the average rubber-bridge player.

All in all, I thought this was quite the best set of entries for the Bols competition, almost all achieving the desired end of enabling a fairly good player to say:

"This I hadn't thought of; this I can do."

INDEX BY SUBJECT

LEADS

PLANNING AHEAD

READING OPPONENTS' HANDS

SIGNALS IN DEFENSE

THIRD HAND PLAY